T0328747

TWO GLASTONBURY LEGENDS:

KING ARTHUR AND ST JOSEPH OF ARIMATHEA

PLATE I

ST JOSEPH OF ARIMATHEA
From Screen at Plymtree, Devon

TWO GLASTONBURY LEGENDS:

KING ARTHUR AND ST JOSEPH OF ARIMATHEA

BY

J. ARMITAGE ROBINSON, D.D., F.B.A.

DEAN OF WELLS

CAMBRIDGE

AT THE UNIVERSITY PRESS

1926

CAMBRIDGE
UNIVERSITY PRESS

University Printing House, Cambridge CB2 8BS, United Kingdom

Cambridge University Press is part of the University of Cambridge.

It furthers the University's mission by disseminating knowledge in the pursuit of
education, learning and research at the highest international levels of excellence.

www.cambridge.org
Information on this title: www.cambridge.org/9781107495142

© Cambridge University Press 1926

First published 1926
First paperback edition 2015

A catalogue record for this publication is available from the British Library

ISBN 978-1-107-49514-2 Paperback

INTRODUCTORY NOTE

THE following pages represent the substance of lectures given on several occasions in response to the enquiry, What is the historical truth underlying the ancient traditions which connect Joseph of Arimathea and King Arthur with the Abbey of Glastonbury? The answer to a question of this kind, if it is to be of any value, demands a patient research and the critical examination of documents. The task is laborious, but it has a peculiar fascination for those who interest themselves in the processes of the medieval mind, who are not content on the one hand to accept traditions as probably true because they were told and believed, or on the other hand to dismiss them at once as what are called monkish tales. History is not merely a record of facts: it has to do with causes and effects, with the development of ideas and the growth of institutions. The first emergence of a tradition, its enrichment by successive generations, its localisation in particular spots—all this concerns the historian, who cannot afford to neglect the gradual growth of any kind of belief. Considered from this point of view the *residuum* of fact which may be shewn to underlie a local tradition is less important than the discovery of the stages through which the tradition has passed, and the causes which appear to have determined its development.

It is in this spirit that I have approached the study of these venerable legends. I have dealt first with King Arthur, because his name is the first to appear in the

documents from which our evidence is drawn. Moreover the full story of Joseph of Arimathea will be found
to be closely bound up with a particular branch of the
Arthurian legend.

It will be convenient here to say a few explanatory
words as to the more important of the writers on
whom we shall have to rely. WILLIAM OF MALMESBURY is
commonly quoted as the principal source of our information. The great historian stayed for a time about the
year 1125 with the monks of Glastonbury. He made a
careful examination of their records, especially their
early charters, and wrote a small treatise *On the
Antiquity of the Church of Glastonbury*. There are
those who have declared that in deference to the feelings
of his kindly hosts he allowed himself to set down their
current traditions without much concern as to their
historical worth. But more recent study has shewn that
the form in which his work has been preserved to us,
in a single manuscript of the middle of the thirteenth
century, is very far from being the form which its author
gave to it. It has been altered and enlarged by a series
of monastic scribes, with the more or less laudable in-
tention of keeping it up to date. It is with the original
form of the book as recovered by critical investigations
that we are in the first instance concerned.

A younger contemporary of William of Malmesbury is GEOFFREY OF MONMOUTH, who about the year
1135 wrote his *History of the Kings of Britain*. This
extraordinary work was declared to be the translation
of a British book: in any case it contains much Celtic
legend in a highly embellished form, and gives us the
first full account of Arthur and his heroic deeds.

Another Welshman was GIRALDUS CAMBRENSIS, a great controversialist and a piquant if not very trustworthy writer, whose literary activity covered some forty years, and who died about 1216.

Two Glastonbury monks are also among our historical authorities: ADAM OF DOMERHAM, who wrote a *History of Glastonbury* in continuation of William of Malmesbury's book down to 1291; and JOHN OF GLASTONBURY who, writing towards the end of the fourteenth century, embodied the works of his two predecessors in a much altered form, and carried on the history to 1342.

It remains only to be said that I am indebted to the kindness of a friend who has facilitated the production of this little book, and also to the skill of Dom Ethelbert Horne of Downside Abbey whose camera has helped to provide the illustrations.

J. ARMITAGE ROBINSON

Easter, 1926

This yet in the meane time pleaseth me, that while we intreate of *Arthure* and of things done by him, *Glastenbury* is alwaies at hand, and most friendly promiseth his endevour towardes assured knowledge of things. From whence in deede all the fruite of our labour at this present is to be fetcht, as it were from a most plentifull running fountaine.

JOHN LELAND

CONTENTS

INTRODUCTORY NOTE   *page* v

KING ARTHUR

§ I. THE EARLY GLASTONBURY TRADITION   I

Pomparlès. William of Malmesbury's evidence as to
(1) the earliest history of Glastonbury; (2) King
Arthur and his end. Geoffrey of Monmouth: Arthur
and Avalon. Caradoc of Llancarvan's *Life of Gildas*.
Giraldus Cambrensis on the discovery of King
Arthur's grave. Adam of Domerham's version of the
same. The plight of Glastonbury after the fire of
1184. St Dunstan's bones. St Patrick's charter. The
site of Avalon.

§ II. THE APPROPRIATION OF HIS STORY   17

Interpolation of William of Malmesbury's book. The
tale of Brent Knoll. John of Glastonbury: Wirral and
Beckery: the miraculous Mass: the change of the
king's arms. The account in *Perceval le Gallois*: 'the
chapel right adventurous.' The English poem of
Libeaus Desconus: 'the pont perilous' by 'the chapel
adventurous' and 'the fair causey.' Pomparlès.

ST JOSEPH OF ARIMATHEA

§ I. THE EARLY TRADITION   28

Additions to William of Malmesbury's book. John of
Glastonbury: (1) Melkin's prophecy; (2) Apocryphal
legends from the Gospel of Nicodemus and the
Passing of Mary; (3) the mission to Britain from 'the
book which is called *The Holy Grail*'; (4) descent of
King Arthur from St Joseph. The genesis of the
tradition. The Grail itself: ignored in the Glastonbury tradition.

ST JOSEPH OF ARIMATHEA (*continued*)

§ II. THE USE MADE OF THE TRADITION   *page* 39
Recapitulation. The great Councils. The *Magna Tabula* at Naworth. The pillar north of the Lady Chapel. *The Lyfe of Joseph of Armathia*: 'Iosephes sherte'; the 'two cruettes'; the miracles of healing. William Good's narrative; uncertainty as to St Joseph's grave; JESUS MARIA; St Joseph's arms; the chapel underground. The value of these venerable traditions.

ADDITIONAL NOTES

I. The Expected Return of King Arthur   51

II. The 'Old Church' at Glastonbury   53

III. The Leaden Cross from King Arthur's Grave, and the Brass Plate from the Column   58

IV. The Grave of St Joseph of Arimathea   60

V. The Two Cruets of St Joseph of Arimathea   65

VI. William Good's Narrative   66

VII. On the Names of some Glastonbury Monks   67

ILLUSTRATIONS

PLATES

I. St Joseph of Arimathea   *Frontispiece*
From Screen at Plymtree, Devon

PAGE

II. Pomparlès   *facing* 1

III. St Joseph of Arimathea   ,, 28
From Window in Langport Church

IV. The *Magna Tabula* at Naworth Castle,
Cumberland   ,, 41
(From *Som. Arch. Soc. Proc.* vol. XXXIV, by permission)

V. The Inscribed Plate from Column north
of Lady Chapel   ,, 43

VI. The Inscription on South Wall of Lady
Chapel   ,, 48

VII. The Shield in stone at Sharpham Manor   ,, 65

IN TEXT

The Leaden Cross from King Arthur's Grave   11

The Second Shield of King Arthur   22

The Arms of St Joseph of Arimathea   49

PLATE II

POMPARLÈS

KING ARTHUR

§ I. THE EARLY GLASTONBURY
TRADITION

WHEN Leland the king's antiquary wandered through Somerset about the year 1542, he found on the river Brue, a mile from Glastonbury, 'a Bridge of Stone of a 4. Arches communely caullid *Pontperlus*, wher men fable that *Arture* cast in his Swerd.' The bridge crosses the river between Glastonbury and Street: in 1415 its Latin name was 'Pons periculosus': to-day, though lately rebuilt, it is still called 'Pomparlès[1].' So Glastonbury not only claimed King Arthur's body, but shewed her pilgrims the very place where he bade farewell to his famous sword.

The story of the successive stages of this appropriation of the Arthurian legend has never been fully told. It may be questioned whether it is possible now to do more than pick up some fragments of it, and assign them to more or less trustworthy dates.

The critical examination of William of Malmesbury's book, *On the Antiquity of the Church of Glastonbury*, enables us at any rate to make a fresh start in the exploration of the subject[2]. We may begin our

---

[1] It is marked as 'Pomperles Bridge' in John Overton's map of Somerset (London, 1668). Our illustration (from Phelps, *Hist. of Somerset*, p. 559) shews the old bridge before 1826. See further in Mr John Morland's articles in *Som. Arch. Soc. Proc.* LVIII, ii, 53; LXVIII, 64.

[2] See *Somerset Historical Essays*, pp. 1–25, where an attempt is made to distinguish between the work of the historian himself and the various additions made to it down to the middle of the thirteenth century.

present enquiry by asking what the historian found
current as to the earliest history of the abbey itself,
and how much of it he was prepared to accept as
reasonably certain tradition, when he was staying for
a time with the monks of Glastonbury about the
year 1125.

First of all, he was ready to believe that the little
church of wattles, dedicated to the Blessed Virgin, was
the most ancient sanctuary of our island, and that it
had been built by the missionaries whom the Pope sent
from Rome at the request of King Lucius in the year
166. He was indeed aware that a yet earlier date was
sometimes claimed for it; that it was even said to have
been built by actual disciples of the Lord. But while
he admitted that, if St Philip had preached in Gaul (as
Freculfus declared), it was not unlikely that he had sent
over missionaries into Britain, he would not commit
himself to a proposition which could be no more than
a pious opinion.

When the great historian was in his grave, his book
was re-edited by more credulous hands. The discovery
had now been made that the Roman missionaries of the
second century whom the Pope had sent to King Lucius,
and whose names had been lost (so William of Malmesbury had said) in the mists of time, were in fact called
Phagan and Deruvian. Moreover they themselves were
not the builders, only the restorers, of the old wattled
church. It had been built by St Philip's missionaries
a century before, and had been dedicated by the Lord
Himself to the honour of His Virgin Mother. So the
legend grew, until at last it came to be believed that the
companions of St Philip had come to our shores under

the leadership of his favourite disciple, Joseph of Arimathea.

Returning to what William of Malmesbury himself has to tell us, we find that he accepts the statement that Gildas the historian of the Britons spent many years at Glastonbury, attracted by the sanctity of this ancient shrine. It was, moreover, a centre of pilgrimage and the resting place of innumerable saints. It was held in high honour by the English conquerors, who spoke of it as the 'Ealde Chirche,' or the Old Church. He gives us a list of names which he read on two 'pyramids' in the monks' cemetery: on one of these were commemorated a Saxon king and bishop, and two Saxon abbots —King Centwine, Bishop Haedde, and the Abbots Bregored and Beorward. He then proceeds to trace the succession of the abbots, so far as their names have been preserved. The first is St Patrick, who, when his work in Ireland was done, spent his last years in Glastonbury and drew the hermits whom he found there into a common monastic life. The fame of St Patrick attracted other Irish saints, such as Bridget and Indract. When he died in 472, he was succeeded by his disciple St Benignus.

Next he tells us, with no token of misgiving, how St David came with seven bishops and would have consecrated the church, but was warned in a dream that the Lord Himself had dedicated it long before. So then, lest he should seem to have come for nought, he built another church and consecrated that.

The Old Church which was built of wattles was said to have been covered with wood by Paulinus, the bishop of Rochester, who had formerly been archbishop of

York. And the historian had seen a very ancient charter by which a king of Domnonia (which then included not only Devon but also the greater part of Somerset) granted to the Old Church land in the isle of Yneswitrin. The king's name was no longer legible; but the abbot of that day was called Worgrez: his name and the names of two other abbots were recorded on a tablet in the Great Church.

This is well-nigh the whole of what William of Malmesbury could find worthy of credence in the story of Glastonbury down to the time when it came under the power of the kings of Wessex (658). After that date indeed he had a new source of information in the charters which recorded a long series of grants by Saxon kings and nobles to the abbots of their day. But for the earlier period he relies on the traditions of the abbey, which he records as traditions for what they may be worth. He adds indeed such confirmation as he can; as when, in regard to St Patrick and St David, he notes that their fame had for centuries brought Irish and Welsh pilgrims to this sacred spot. The general method of his work makes it practically certain that he had never heard the name of Joseph of Arimathea in connexion with Glastonbury, nor indeed the name of King Arthur.

It will be well at this point to ask how much William of Malmesbury can, from his other writings, be shewn to have known of King Arthur and his story. In the *Gesta Regum* he says that after the death of Vortimer—the valiant opponent of the Saxon invaders who had entered the country at the invitation of his father the unworthy Vortigern—the Britons would have come utterly to nought but for their new king Ambrosius, the sole survivor of the Romans, who kept the Saxons in check through the notable efforts of the warlike Arthur. 'This is the Arthur,' he continues, 'concerning whom the idle tales of the Britons rave wildly even to-day: a man certainly worthy to be celebrated not in the foolish dreams of deceitful fables, but in truthful history; since for a long time he sustained the declining fortunes of his country, and incited the unbroken spirit of the people to war; and finally, at the siege of Mount Badon, relying on the figure of the Lord's Mother which he had embroidered on his armour, he attacked nine hundred of the enemy himself alone and put them to flight with incredible slaughter[1].' The story of this battle comes out of Nennius; but William of Malmesbury seems to have heard more of King Arthur than the earlier historian relates, though he is not willing to repeat what he accounts mere fables.

In a later passage of the *Gesta Regum* he speaks of Gawain, and says that

some years ago, in the province of Wales called Ros, there was discovered the tomb of Walwen, who being the son of Arthur's sister was not unworthy of him. He ruled in that part of Britain which is still called Walweitha: a very valiant knight, but he was driven from his kingdom by the brother and nephew of Hengist; first getting satisfaction, however, by inflicting great harm upon them. He shared deservedly in the glory of his uncle, because they deferred for many years the ruin of their falling country. The sepulchre of Arthur is nowhere known; whence ancient songs fable that he will come again. But the tomb of the other, as I have just said, was discovered in the time of K. William upon the shore of the sea, fourteen feet in length; where it

[1] *G.R.* I, II f.

is said by some that he was wounded by enemies, and ship-wrecked; by others, that he was killed by his countrymen at a public feast. The truth, therefore remains in doubt, but neither of them was unworthy of his fame[1].

Thus far William of Malmesbury: and though he is held to have revised his *Gesta Regum* in 1140 shortly before his death—inserting into it considerable portions of the book *On the Antiquity of Glastonbury* which he had written since the first edition had come out—there is nothing to shew that on any of the points that have come before us he had acquired fresh information or had changed his view. Yet in the meantime Geoffrey of Monmouth had published his *History of the Kings of Britain*, which claimed to be the translation into Latin of a British book, and which by its brilliant invention lifted the Arthurian legend into a new region of literary romance.

We have, then, next to ask whether Geoffrey of Monmouth says anything that connects the legend of King Arthur with Glastonbury. At first sight it might seem that he does; and doubtless later writers interpreted him to this effect. For he relates that, when the king was 'mortally wounded' in the battle on the river Cambula in Cornwall, 'he was carried thence to the isle of Avalon for the healing of his wounds[2].'

Here no hint is given as to where the isle of Avalon was supposed to be, but in the *Life of Merlin*, a Latin poem of Geoffrey's time and claiming to be written by Geoffrey himself, the bard Taliesson is made to describe the voyage of the wounded king at much greater

---

[1] *G.R.* II, 342.   [2] *History* XI, 2.

length. The island to which he is taken is not actually called by the name of Avalon, but it is

The Isle of Apples, called the Fortunate Isle.

Here there is no tilling of the soil: nature unassisted brings forth her corn and fruits: life is extended to a hundred years and more. Nine sisters gently rule this Happy Land. The eldest, Morgen, is the fairest and the most skilled. She knows how to change her shape and fly like Daedalus whither she may desire. In medicine too she is supreme. To her the king is brought, and she probes his wound, and at last declares that he will recover, if he will abide a long time under her care.

We have no ground, therefore, for supposing that Geoffrey identified the isle of Avalon with Glastonbury. That this identification was of primary importance goes without saying: but we shall have to look elsewhere to find the first traces of it.

There is a *Life of Gildas*, written by Caradoc of Llancarvan, a contemporary of Geoffrey of Monmouth, which in a story near the close brings King Arthur to Glastonbury. The wicked King Melwas, of 'the summer region' (i.e. Somerset), had carried off Arthur's wife Guennuvar, and held her in this safe stronghold. King Arthur brought up the whole forces of Cornwall and Devon to effect her release: the abbot of Glastonbury, accompanied by St Gildas, intervened to prevent a conflict, and peaceable restoration of the queen was thus secured. Here then Arthur comes to Glastonbury: but, though the writer can tell us that the 'City of Glass' derives its name from the British Yniswitrin, he gives no hint that it was identical with the island of Avalon[1].

It would seem that the earliest record in literature of the identification of Avalon with Glastonbury comes from the pen of Giraldus Cambrensis. In his book *De Principis Instructione*[2] he speaks of King Arthur as having had a special devotion to St Mary of Glastonbury, of whose church he was a generous patron, and whose image he painted on his shield and kissed its feet in the hour of battle. Of Arthur's body, he continues, fanciful tales were told: as that it was carried off by spirits to remote regions, and was not subject to death. But 'in our times' it was discovered buried deep in the earth, in a hollowed oak, between two stone pyramids in the cemetery of Glastonbury. A leaden cross was found, fixed to the under part of a stone in such a way that the inscription was turned inwards. The writer had himself seen it, and gives the words as follows: 'Hic jacet sepultus inclitus rex Arthurus cum Wenneveria uxore sua secunda in insula Avallonia.' Two-thirds of the sepulchre contained the bones of the king, the remainder those of his wife at his feet: a yellow lock of the queen's hair turned to dust when touched by a too eager monk. Some indications that King Arthur would be found there the brethren had gathered from writings which they possessed; others from letters carved on the pyramids; others again through visions and revelations made to

---

[1] This *Life of Gildas* is edited by Mommsen in *M.H.G. Auct. Antiquiss*, XIII, i, 107 ff.

[2] VIII, 126 ff. (Rolls Ser. edn). This portion of the work is thought to have been written *c.* 1194.

some of their number. But above all King Henry had plainly told them the whole matter as he had heard it from an ancient historical poet of the Britons—how that deep down, sixteen feet at least below the ground, they should find the body, not in a marble tomb, but in a hollowed oak. The secrecy of this deep burial, with the letters on the cross concealed, was due to a desire to hide the body from his old enemies the Saxons.

Giraldus goes on to say that what is now called 'Glastonia' was anciently called 'insula Avalonia': for it is an island surrounded by marshes; wherefore in the British language it is named Inis Avalon, that is 'insula pomifera': for at one time it abounded in apples, for which the British word is 'aval.' Morganis, a noble matron who was ruler and patron of those parts and allied by blood to King Arthur, carried him away after the battle of Kemale for the healing of his wounds to the island now called 'Glastonia.' It had also formerly been called in the British tongue 'Inis gutrin,' that is 'insula vitrea': and from this name the Saxons who came afterwards called the place 'Glastingeburi': for 'glas' in their language is the same as 'vitrum,' and 'buri' is 'castrum' or 'civitas.'

King Arthur's bones were of enormous size. His shin-bone came some distance above the knee of the tallest man in the place; his head was prodigiously large, and it had ten wounds or more, all of which had healed up, save a gaping one which seemed to indicate the death-blow.

Some twenty-five years later Giraldus told the story again in his *Speculum Ecclesiae*[1]. He begins by dating

[1] IV, 47 ff.

the incident in the reign of King Henry II, and in the time of Abbot Henry, who was afterwards bishop of Worcester. He speaks of the cemetery as having been dedicated by St Dunstan; and he enlarges on the beauty of the yellow lock of hair, and says that the imprudent monk jumped into the deep grave to handle it; and he draws a moral about monks and ladies' hair.

He then tells the 'true story' of King Arthur's death as before, to confute the fables of the Britons, who look for his return as the Jews expect their Messiah. He repeats his etymological notes, adding however that possibly Avallonia may be derived, not from 'aval,' an apple, but from Avallon a former ruler of the island[1]. Most of what he had said before is given here again, but there is no mention of the size of the king's bones.

Such is the tale as Giraldus tells it. We need not press the anachronism of his second narrative, which makes Henry de Sully (who was appointed by King Richard in 1189) to be the abbot of King Henry's time. The most probable date for the discovery is that given by Ralph de Coggeshall, writing about the time of Giraldus's first account. Under the year 1191 he records the finding of King Arthur's bones, when a grave was being dug for a monk who had specially desired to be buried between the two pyramids. He gives the inscription on the leaden cross, but without the mention of Queen Guinevere.

It is to be noted that the words 'cum Wenneveria

---

[1] The text is given as 'a Vallone quodam': but John of Glastonbury (p. 10), who has borrowed from the passage, has 'ab Avallone quodam.'

uxore sua secunda' are peculiar to Giraldus. He gives them in both his accounts, though in the first case before and in the second case after 'in insula Avallonia.' He expressly says that he read them himself. But no two persons seem to have read the inscription quite in the same way. Leland had the cross in his hands (*c.* 1540) and measured it; and he gives the words thus: 'hic jacet sepultus inclitus rex Arturius in insula Avalonia[1].' Another writer, who saw it with his own eyes, gives it thus: 'Hic jacet gloriosissimus rex Britonum Arturus[2].'

Cross from King
Arthur's Grave

The official Glastonbury account is given by Adam of Domerham (*c.* 1290). After speaking of the accession of Henry de Sully, who had been appointed by King Richard, he says (p. 341):

This abbot having been frequently admonished concerning the more honourable placing of the famous King

---

[1] Leland's *Assertio Arturii*, quoted by Ussher, *Antiqq.* (ed. 1687), p. 63. Leland elsewhere says that King Arthur's tomb was in the midst of the presbytery, with King Edward the Elder on the north and Edward Ironside on the south. The cross lay on the tomb (*Itin.* III, 63; *Som. Arch. Soc. Proc.* XXXIII, ii, 103 f.). See further in Additional Note III.

[2] See Ussher, l.c.

Arthur—for he had rested near the Old Church between two stone pyramids, nobly engraved in former times, for six hundred and forty eight years—on a certain day set curtains round the spot and gave orders to dig. When they had dug to an immense depth and were almost in despair, they found a wooden sarcophagus of wondrous size, enclosed on every side. When they had raised and opened it they found the king's bones, which were incredibly large, so that one shin-bone reached from the ground to the middle of a tall man's leg, and even further. They found also a leaden cross, having on one side the inscription: 'Hic jacet sepultus inclitus rex Arturius in insula Avallonia.' After this they opened the tomb of the queen who was buried with Arthur, and found a fair yellow lock of woman's hair plaited with wondrous art; but when they touched it, it crumbled almost to nothing. [He goes on to speak of the re-interment in the Great Church.]

This account is sober enough[1]: in fact it was too dull for a scribe who was almost contemporary with Adam of Domerham, and who added in the margin of the manuscript the more interesting story which he drew from Giraldus Cambrensis, and gave the words of the inscription with the addition of Queen Guinevere's name as in the *Speculum Ecclesiae*. If we add 648 to 542, the year assigned to King Arthur's death, we get 1190 as the official Glastonbury date of the discovery.

What are we to make of the story in this its simplest and most authentic form? We must first glance at the history of the abbey, to see if that casts any light upon it. Henry of Blois, the bishop of Winchester, had died on 9 August 1171. During forty-five years he had ruled the abbey of Glastonbury, and had added

---

[1] It is in part drawn from Giraldus's *Speculum Ecclesiae*, which however it corrects at several points.

much to its property and magnificence. After some delay a new abbot was appointed to succeed him, but at Easter 1180 a fresh vacancy occurred, and the king was glad to keep the abbey in his hands and to draw the revenues, which amounted to the great sum of £500 a year. Then on St Urban's day, 25 May 1184, the whole monastery was consumed by fire. It was a loss which could not be reckoned in terms of money; for the oldest church in this land had perished, the little sanctuary built of twisted wattles by the first British Christians. No new buildings, however splendid, could restore the prestige which had made Glastonbury the centre of pilgrimages, 'the second Rome.' The monks did what they could to collect the bones of their buried saints. They dug up Patrick and Indract and Gildas, and others whose places of burial were well known. Then to their immense consolation it transpired that one of their number knew the hiding-place of the bones of St Dunstan, which had been brought—so they claimed—from Canterbury when it lay deserted after the murder of St Alphege by the Danes. The wrath of the Canterbury monks of a later day, who denied their claim, had been so great that it was no longer safe to exhibit their treasure: so it was secretly built into a wall of the church, and thenceforth one monk only in any generation was allowed to know the spot: as he neared his end he entrusted his secret to the most prudent of his brethren. Now in the hour of their deepest need the secret was disclosed, and the precious deposit was recovered from the ruins[1].

[1] So at the present day the Benedictine monks pass on the secret of what is held to be the true resting-place of St Cuthbert in the Cathedral Church of Durham.

The king did his part with unusual generosity. He placed the whole of the revenues at the disposal of Ralph fitz Stephen, his chamberlain, who began the rebuilding on the most magnificent scale. First rose the beautiful new chapel of Our Lady, where the Old Church had stood throughout the centuries; and this was consecrated within a few years by Bishop Reginald. Meantime a vast church was planned to the east of this, and part of it was ready for use a few years later. But King Henry died in the summer of 1189. The financial position was suddenly reversed. King Richard, eager to gather monies for the Crusade, filled every vacant post for a due consideration. Though the new abbot of Glastonbury, Henry de Sully, was his nephew, he doubtless entered upon his abbacy with a heavy load of debt: at any rate 'he lent no helping hand to the building'; and the monks in their distress sent preachers round the country with relics and indulgences in the hope of gathering the necessary funds. It was at this moment that the valuable discovery was made that between the two pyramids south of the Lady Chapel lay King Arthur and his queen.

Yet darker days were in store for the monks of Glastonbury. Savary, the new bishop of Bath, got Henry de Sully promoted to the see of Worcester in 1193, and after a long struggle secured the abbacy for himself, taking the double title of Bishop of Bath and Glastonbury. It was a full quarter of a century before the monks could extricate themselves from the bonds of this 'tyranny,' and the costs of their incessant pleading at the papal court must have been a serious strain on their resources.

But their imaginations were quickened by their troubles, and new revelations enhanced the glory of their inheritance. A charter of St Patrick was found in St Michael's Chapel on the Tor, having escaped the fire owing to the far-seeing wisdom of the saint who had written it in duplicate. Here was the whole story of St Phagan and St Deruvian, as well as St Patrick's account of his own doings, and promises of indulgence on an unexampled scale[1]. William of Malmesbury's book *On the Antiquity of Glastonbury* had to be brought up to date; for he had not even known the names of the two missionaries whom King Lucius had obtained from Rome: nor had he spoken of King Arthur and the isle of Avalon. Several fresh chapters had to be written, on some of which the marks of the Great Fire are plain to be seen. And before the book reached the final state in which it has come down to us, a new first chapter was composed, in which occurs the earliest mention of St Joseph of Arimathea.

At this point a question arises which tempts us to a short digression. If King Arthur first appears in connexion with Glastonbury when his bones were 'discovered' in 1191, what had suggested the search for them there?

Giraldus says that King Henry had learned of his burial at Glastonbury from Welsh bards. But we have no more than his statement (which involves an anachronism) for thinking that King Henry concerned himself at all in the matter.

We must go back to Geoffrey of Monmouth. He says in his *History of the Kings of Britain* that after

---

[1] See *Somerset Historical Essays*, pp. 15 ff.

the battle in Cornwall Arthur was brought to Avalon
for the healing of his wounds. This is all he can or will
say of his end. Now William of Malmesbury had said
a few years before that King Arthur's burial-place
was unknown, and hence the Britons fabled that he
would come again. Geoffrey neither accepts nor rejects
this belief. Nor does he tell us where Avalon is.

There can be little doubt that the legend of Arthur's
end originally implied that he was supernaturally re-
moved to a Better Land, an Isle of the Blest, where his
wounds should be healed, and whence in the future
he might return to his own people[1]. Such a legend
seems to underlie the popular belief that Arthur and
his knights lie somewhere in a magic sleep, awaiting
the day of the return: more than one place lays claim
to such a legend; and this fact in itself suggests that
the place from the outset was a mysterious one[2].

What then of Avalon? Was it a known locality at
all? Or was it a name for the Celtic Paradise? Now
Geoffrey, as we have seen, gives us no hint as to where
it may be situated. The same vagueness surrounds
Avalon in the early romances which followed Geoffrey's lead toward the end of the twelfth century. It
is in the far west, or even in the Antipodes.

Yet we can hardly doubt that the monks searched
for King Arthur's body in their cemetery because
Glastonbury was already supposed by local tradition
to be the Avalon to which the wounded hero had been
brought. The great Tor, rising solitary and steep out

---

[1] This is quite clearly the view of the author of the *Vita Merlini*
already referred to.
[2] See Additional Note I.

of the watery moors, must needs have been an island of mystery from the prehistoric days when the lake-dwellers clustered round its base. Long before the first Christian settlers came it must have had its store of legend. It has been suggested that it was the Island of King Avallon or Avalloc (*Ynys Avallach* as the Welsh versions write the name)—a deity perchance of the underworld: that it was the stronghold of Eurawc (or Evelake) of the Peredur story in the Mabinogion which lies behind the Perceval romance. These are points which we must leave to the Celtic scholars who alone are qualified for their determination. But we may not unreasonably suppose that the name of Avalon was not first suggested by the inventiveness of monks; that it represented some primitive tradition, and had clung to the spot in the popular memory, in spite of the coming of Christianity and in spite of successive conquests of the land by Saxon and Norman invaders.

The problem is indeed outside the immediate scope of our enquiry. Our task has been the simpler one of tracing the Arthurian legend back as far as our Glastonbury records take us; and we can say with practical certainty that the claim of the monks to Avalon and to King Arthur's grave was not put forward before the year 1191.

§ II. THE APPROPRIATION OF HIS STORY

We shall now proceed to enquire what use Glastonbury has made of the story of King Arthur, and how it

R   2

has linked it up with certain localities in the neighbourhood.

An interpolator of the *De Antiquitate*, not later than the middle of the thirteenth century, says (p. 43):

Arthur, in the year of the Lord's Incarnation 542, was wounded fatally by Modred in Cornwall, near the river Camba; and thence he was carried for the healing of his wounds to the island of Avallon; and there he died in the summer, about Pentecost, being well nigh a hundred years old or thereabout.

A marginal note, added by a hand not much later, is merely derived from Giraldus Cambrensis (*Spec. Eccl.* p. 48), and need not be given here.

Then on p. 47 we have an interpolated section headed *De illustri Arturo*. This records, as from *The Deeds of King Arthur*, the story of Ider, son of King Nuth, whom Arthur knighted one Christmas at Karliun. He took him with him to fight against three giants in the Mount of Frogs, now called Brent Knoll. The young knight managed to get ahead by himself, fought the giants and slew them. When Arthur came up he found Ider in a state of collapse and apparently dead: he left the body till a cart should be sent to fetch it. Regarding himself as responsible for his death, he went to Glastonbury and there appointed eighty monks to pray for his soul, and gave possessions and lands for their sustenance, with other precious gifts in abundance.

An early marginal note here says 'To wit Brent, which was thus set free, and Poldon with the neighbouring lands.' The same early hand has added at the beginning of this section:

For Arthur, see the ninth book of the Brut concerning his deeds, and for his coronation, &c., books ten and eleven. For the prophecies of Merlin see the seventh book of the same. And how he was begotten you will find in the end of the sixth[1] book.

The same story about Ider is told by John of Glastonbury (p. 76): but he places the scene of it in North Wales, in the Mount of Spiders (*in Monte de Areynes*, instead of *in Monte Ranarum*); and at the end he says: 'For he gave Brent Marsh and Pouldon, and many other properties, which afterwards the pagan Saxons when they occupied this land took away, but subsequently being converted to the faith of Christ they restored them.' This account enables us to trace the growth of the legend. Though written later, it is evidently more original than the other. It forms part of a long narrative about King Arthur. There is no mention of Brent Knoll, which indeed was much too far from Caerleon to come into the story of the giants; though Brent Marsh is mentioned at the end as among King Arthur's penitential gifts to Glastonbury.

We now pass on from the interpolators of William of Malmesbury's book and come to John of Glastonbury's *History*. Here we have (p. 73) an account of King Arthur, beginning with his birth at Tintagel and his accession at the age of fifteen in the tenth year of Cedric. His descent from Joseph of Arimathea is given for a second time. Then the history of Gildas is told, including an account of his elder brother Hueil, whom Arthur slew for ravaging the land[2]. Gildas hereupon returned

---

[1] This should be the 'eighth,' the reference being to Geoffrey of Monmouth's *History of the Kings of Britain*.

[2] This comes in the *Life of Gildas* by Caradoc of Llancarvan.

from Ireland, and visited the king, who expressed sorrow for his deed and was forgiven. After this we are told that Arthur fought the Saxons in twelve battles and overcame them: yet Cedric became even more threatening, until Arthur accepted his homage and gave him Hampshire and Somerset, which he called Wessex[1]. Then follows the Ider story already noticed. The story which comes next has several local touches, and must be told with some fulness:

There was at that time in Wirral within the island of Avallonia a monastery of holy virgins, dedicated in the name of the Apostle Peter, wherein Arthur oftentimes rested and abode, attracted by the amenity of the place. Now it came to pass at a certain time that the king was staying there and sleeping in his chamber; and there came to him an angel of the Lord and said, 'Arthur, Arthur.' And he awoke and said, 'Who art thou?' The angel answered, 'It is I who speak with thee. At break of day arise and go to the hermitage of St Mary Magdalen of Bekeri in this island: behold and understand what there shall be done.' The king arose in the morning and told the vision to a knight of his named Gawayn. But he suggested to his lord the king that it was of no account. The angel appeared again the second night, and the king determined that if a third summons should come it must be obeyed.

As the shades of night drew on, the king bade his attendant (*simmistam*) to be ready in the morning to set forth with him to the hermitage. (Here something has been omitted.) And he (i.e. the attendant), entering the chapel, beheld there a corpse on a bier, and four candles standing on this side and on that, after the manner of the monks; and on the altar two golden candlesticks. Stirred by avarice he seized one of these and hid it wickedly beneath his cloak—a thing which

[1] The statement may have been taken over from Higden's *Polychronicon*, c. 6.

the issue proved to have been ill done. When he would go forth from the chapel, there met him one who, chiding him withal for sacrilege, smote him in the groin. Grievously wounded he cried aloud even as a madman. The king awoke, and in great fear sought what this might be: he rose up and went forth at once to the bed of his attendant, demanding what had come to him. He told the thing in order to the king, shewed him the candlestick in his cloak and the weapon in his groin, and expired; and he was buried among the nuns in Wirral. In testimony whereof, as it is said, the candlestick and the knife remain in the treasury of the king of England at Westminster unto this day.

The king therefore, perceiving that God would have none enter that chapel save for his soul's salvation, as soon as it was dawn maketh his way thither alone. And as he drew near the chapel, lo, two hands holding swords on either side of the door, that smote against each other, and struck out fire, as it were lightning, before the king's eyes. Smitten with great fear he bethought him what he should do, since so holy a place he might not enter. Then falling on his knees he besought the Lord to shew him mercy and make him worthy to enter therein. (His prayer was granted.) And seeing that the swords were gone he entered the holy place, which was adorned beyond compare. There met him a venerable old man, clad in black robes, with a long beard and white hair; and he saluted the king. And he, humbly returning the salutation, set himself at one side of the chapel to see the end. He saw all that his servant had related. The old man now began to vest himself in priestly robes; and forthwith there came the glorious Mother of the Lord, bearing her Son in her arms, and began to serve the old man. But when he began the Mass and came as far as to the offertory, Our Lady offered to the priest her Son. The priest set Him on the corporal next the chalice. And when he came to the immolation of the Host, that is, to the Lord's words 'This is My Body,' he elevated the Boy in his hands. King Arthur stood for that Sacrament of the Lord, nay for the Lord Himself, and made suppliant adoration. The old man, after this immolation of the Boy, set Him where He was before. When he came to the reception of the Host, he took and received and ate that Boy, the Son of God, according to the institution of the Lord who said 'Take and eat.' When He had been received and the communion made, He appeared in the same place as before, sitting unharmed and entire, the spotless paschal Lamb. When the whole divine office was completed, Our Lady, the glorious Mother, in testimony of all this gave to the king a crystal cross, which to this day, by gift of the same king, is honourably kept and preserved in the treasury of Glastonbury, and year by year in Lent is carried in procession on Wednesdays and Fridays: for on Wednesday was the marvel done, even on Ash Wednesday. Then she took back her Son, and they passed out of sight. [The old man interpreted all this to the king, and explained that the corpse in the chapel was that of a brother hermit from Andredesey, who had come to visit him and had fallen sick and died. The king repented him of his sins and made vows of contrition to Our Lady and her Son our Lord Jesus.] His arms also he changed in their honour. For whereas they were silver, with three lions red, turning their heads to their backs, from the time of the coming of Brutus even until this change of King Arthur;

now, in memory of the crystal cross given him by the Blessed Mary, he made them to be green, with a cross of silver; and over the right arm of the cross, in memory of the miracle aforesaid, he set the image of Blessed Mary ever Virgin, holding her Son in her arms. And the king bade farewell to the old man, being confirmed in the faith of the Lord, and went from strength to strength, and was mightily rejoiced.

If now we turn to the romance of *Perceval le Gallois*, rendered into English by the late Sebastian Evans under the title of *The High History of the Holy Grail*, we find at the outset this same story in a wholly different setting. King Arthur has fallen into slackness and despair, and the knights are deserting his court. Queen Guinevere at last persuades him to go to the chapel of St Augustine in the White Forest, which 'may not be found save by adventure only.' The king consents and she declares again: 'The place is right perilous and the chapel right adventurous. But the most worshipful hermit that is in the kingdom of Wales hath his dwelling beside the chapel.' The king would have gone alone, but the queen insists that he shall at least take one squire: he chooses a youth named Chaus.

The story is then told with some difference of detail, and the stolen candlestick is given 'to St Paul in London, for the church was newly founded.' After the incident which was fatal to the squire, the king starts by himself. The chapel where the corpse of the knight (not of the hermit) lies, and whence the candlestick was taken, is now the scene of a conflict for the dead man's soul, which is only rescued from the demons by Our Lady's intervention. The king has still to go forward and seek the chapel of St Augustine. Here at length, though he cannot enter, he beholds the wondrous Mass. But he receives no crystal cross, nor does he change the arms on his shield.

Both stories come from a common source. The Glastonbury one is the less highly developed, and is no doubt a local recension of what the monks found in their book which was called *The Deeds of King Arthur*. The king's starting-place is not, as in the Perceval romance, the great hall at Cardoil, but a convent of St Peter on Wirral, the hilly ridge to the south-west of Glastonbury. The 'chapel right adventurous' is not St Augustine's in the White Forest, where dwells the holiest hermit of Wales. It is but half a mile west of Glastonbury, down on the edge of the moor—the chapel of St Mary Magdalen. If no trace can now be found of St Peter's nunnery on Wirral, we are more fortunate as regards this chapel. Beckery, or Little Ireland, as the name signifies, was the traditional resort of St Bridget, who dwelt there for many years, and on her return to her own country left her wallet, bell and weaving instruments behind, with other memorials of her stay. The name survives unchanged in *Beckery Mill*, and the fields adjoining are still known as *Brides*[1]. There too, hidden beneath the grass, are the foundations of St Bridget's Chapel. They were dug out some forty years ago[2]. Within the outer lines of the rectangular building were the foundations of a much earlier and smaller chapel. This agrees well enough with the statement of John of Glastonbury that the chapel on Beckery island was first dedicated to St Mary Magdalen, and later to St Bridget. North of the site

[1] The place was called *Bride-hay*, according to a MS quoted by Ussher, *ut supra*, p. 467.
[2] See Mr John Morland's article in *Som. Arch. Soc. Proc.* xxxv, li, 121 ff.

are the foundations of a priest's house as large as the later chapel itself.

A further local touch is given by changing the dead knight of the Perceval story into a dead hermit from the island of Andredesey. This island is the furthest western limit of the Twelve Hides: its earliest name was Edred's Island. It is now called Nyland, and forms a little civil parish to itself between Rodney Stoke and Cheddar[1].

Lastly we note that the gift of the crystal cross is prettily introduced as offering an explanation of the heraldic shield of Glastonbury Abbey—*Vert, a cross botonnée arg., on a canton of the last the Virgin and Child*.

Thus much at the moment for 'the chapel right adventurous.' We pass on half a mile, skirting the slopes of Wirral, and find ourselves once more at *Pomparlès*, the Perilous Bridge, of which we spoke at the outset. This bridge is on the causey which leads across the river Brue and over the moor to Street. How came it by this curious name?

The English poem of *Libeaus Desconus* corresponds to the French romance entitled *Le Bel Inconnu* by Renauld de Beaujeu[2]. Its opening story runs as follows:

A youth whose mother brings him up in retirement, and will not let him know his name or parentage (he is Gingelain, son of Gawain), finds a dead knight and donning his armour goes to King Arthur's court at Glastonbury. Though he is laughed at for a child, Arthur makes him a knight and grants him as a boon that the first adventure that is called for shall be his. A maiden with a dwarf appears and pleads for the

[1] See *Som. and Dors. Notes and Queries*, XVIII, 74.
[2] I owe the reference to this poem in the first instance to Mr John Morland's article in *Som. Arch. Soc. Proc.* LVIII, ii, 58.

release of a captive lady in an enchanted castle. Libeaus Desconus—the Fair Unknown, for so Arthur has named him—claims the errand. The maiden scorns him, and the dwarf pleads with the king not to allow it, as many grievous battles must be expected:

> The dwerf with greet errour
> Wente to king Arthour
>   And seide: 'Kinde king!
> This child to be werrour
> And do swich a labour
>   Is nought worth a ferthing.
> Er he that lady se
> He schall do batailes thre
>   With oute any lesing.
> At the point perilous,
> Be the chapell auntrous,
>   Shall be his beginning.'

A later recension has 'at the bridge of perill,' and 'besyde the adventurous chapell.' The youth insists on his claim: he is armed by the foremost knights, and blessed by King Arthur. Then they set forth:

> They ride forth all thre
> Upon a faire causé,
>   Be the chapell auntrous.
> The knight they gonne y-se
> In armes bright of ble[1]
>   Upon the point perilous.

Here is a variant 'pont perilous'; as also 'bridge of perill' in the later recension.

In the French romance, instead of Glastonbury as the scene of the king's court, we find 'Charlion qui siet sor mer,' that is, Caerleon on the Severn Sea; and instead of the perilous bridge 'le gue perilleus' (that is, the

[1] i.e. 'colour.'

perilous ford). It is no mere coincidence that in a single stanza of the English poem we have the Fair Causey, the Chapel Adventurous, and the Bridge Perilous; and moreover that the starting point is the king's court at Glastonbury.

The English poem is dated by Max Kaluza in the second quarter of the fourteenth century[1]. Some eighty years later (1415) we get our earliest mention of the 'Pons Periculosus' in the Glastonbury records.

So we end this part of our enquiry where we began—at the 'Bridge of Stone of a 4. Arches communely caullid *Pontperlus*, wher men fable that *Arture* cast in his Swerd.' Of all the claims that we have been faced with, this about the sword is perhaps the most amazing. We have only Leland's word for it, and need not attribute so futile a suggestion to the monks: he probably picked it up at his inn, when he visited the place a second time, some few years after the dissolution of the abbey. But it serves as evidence that *Pomparlès* was somehow connected with the Arthurian legend, though the true story of the connexion, as we are now able to tell it, was not popularly known.

[1] See *Libeaus Desconus*, edited by Max Kaluza, Leipzig, 1890, p. clxvi.

ST JOSEPH OF ARIMATHEA

§ I. THE EARLY TRADITION

OF Joseph of Arimathea, as we have already said, William of Malmesbury knows nothing. But in the introductory chapter by another hand, prefixed to the *De Antiquitate* in the middle of the thirteenth century, we hear for the first time that at the head of the twelve disciples whom St Philip sent over from Gaul he placed, as it is said (*ut ferunt*), Joseph of Arimathea. We are further told that the pagan king to whom they came was not willing to accept their teaching, yet as they had come from far he gave them the island of Yniswitrin. Afterwards he and two other kings in succession gave each of them a portion of land; and these portions afterwards came to be known as the Twelve Hides. At the bidding of the archangel Gabriel they built a church of wattles in honour of the Blessed Mary, thirty-one years after the Passion of our Lord and fifteen after the Assumption of the Virgin. This was the first church in the land, and it was dedicated to His Mother by the Lord Himself. After these first disciples had fallen asleep, the place was deserted until the days of King Lucius, when the chapel was discovered and repaired by Phagan and Deruvian, the missionaries from Rome. The story had been told thus, as we have seen, in St Patrick's charter—the only new point made here being the bare mention of Joseph of Arimathea as the leader of the original band.

A long marginal note to the first original section of

PLATE III

ST JOSEPH OF ARIMATHEA
From Window in Langport Church

the *De Antiquitate*, added by an early hand, says: 'That Joseph of Arimathea, the noble counsellor, with his son Josephes and many others, came to Greater Britain (which is now called Anglia) and there ended his life, is attested by the book of *The Deeds of the famous King Arthur*.' For this statement reference is made to 'the Quest of Lancelot de Lac,' and to 'the Quest of the vessel which there they call the Holy Grail.' Another early note says: 'For this chapter see the whole of the fourth book, and most of the fifth, of the Brut (*Bruti*).' The reference here is to the *Historia Regum Britanniae* of Geoffrey of Monmouth (capp. iv, v.).

So much for the *De Antiquitate* in its latest and most expanded form. Our next authority is John of Glastonbury, from whom we may see the extraordinary amplification of the story which had taken place before the end of the fourteenth century. His book was published by Hearne in 1726; and copies of it are now so rare outside the great libraries that we shall be justified in giving a somewhat full account of what he has to tell us in this connexion.

First, we note that he had before him the enlarged edition of the *De Antiquitate*, just as we have it to-day; for he states in his prologue that William of Malmesbury wrote an account of the abbey 'from the coming of St Joseph' down to the time of Henry of Blois; but, as we have seen, the coming of St Joseph is only barely mentioned, with an *ut ferunt*, in the introductory chapter which belongs to the latest stage of the enlargement.

After he has given the Bounds of the Twelve Hides, he goes on to speak of 'the Saints who rest in the

church of Glastonbury' (p. 16). Here, after embodying
a few sentences from *De Antiq.*, p. 27, he inserts at the
head of the list Joseph of Arimathea and his son Josephes.
On p. 29, after a few lines from William of Malmesbury
(*De Antiq.*, p. 42), he comes back to the subject of
burials, and quotes a prophecy of Melkin the British
bard. This is a queer piece of semi-poetical prose,
intended to mystify and hardly capable of translation
into English[1].

> Avalon's island, with avidity
> Claiming the death of pagans,
> More than all in the world beside,
> For the entombment of them all,
> Honoured by chanting spheres of prophecy:
> And for all time to come
> Adornèd shall it be
> By them that praise the Highest.
> Abbadarè, mighty in Saphat,
> Noblest of pagans,
> With countless thousands
> There hath fallen on sleep.
> Amid these Joseph in marble,
> Of Arimathea by name,
> Hath found perpetual sleep:
> And he lies on a two-forked line
> Next the south corner of an oratory
> Fashioned of wattles
> For the adoring of a mighty Virgin
> By the aforesaid sphere-betokened
> Dwellers in that place, thirteen in all.
> For Joseph hath with him
> In his sarcophagus
> Two cruets, white and silver,

---

[1] For the Latin see Additional Note IV.

Filled with blood and sweat
Of the Prophet Jesus.
When his sarcophagus
Shall be found entire, intact,
In time to come, it shall be seen
And shall be open unto all the world:
Thenceforth nor water nor the dew of heaven
Shall fail the dwellers in that ancient isle.
For a long while before
The day of judgement in Josaphat
Open shall these things be
And declared to living men.

Of this supposed pagan prophecy we shall have to say
something later, especially in connexion with the *duo
fassula,*—the 'two cruettes' of the metrical *Lyfe of
Joseph of Armathia*[1].

After this John of Glastonbury goes on to speak of
King Coel, Caradoc of Cornwall, King Arthur, and a
host of others. Then (p. 48) we are given 'a Treatise
concerning Joseph of Arimathea, drawn from a certain book, which the Emperor Theodosius found at
Jerusalem in Pilate's Judgement Hall.' This title guides
us at once to the early apocryphal book known by the
name of *Gesta Pilati*, or the Gospel of Nicodemus. This
work had long been popular in England, and an Anglo-
Saxon version of part of it goes back, it is said, to the
beginning of the eleventh century. From this book we
are now given an extract, which contains all that is
there related as to Joseph of Arimathea. It may be
summarised as follows:

The Jews, hearing that Joseph had buried the body of
Jesus, sought to take him and Nicodemus and certain

[1] See Additional Notes IV and V.

others. When the rest fled, Joseph and Nicodemus presented themselves, justifying their action and reproaching the Jews for their ingratitude. The Jews shut up Joseph in a windowless cell, sealed the door and set a guard. When they opened the cell he was not there. It was presently (after the Ascension) found that he was in his own city of Arimathea. The high priests were rejoiced at the discovery, and sent a letter of invitation by some of his friends, asking him to come in peace. On his return to Jerusalem they asked him to explain how he got away. Four angels had lifted the cell into the air, whilst he stood in prayer; and the Lord had appeared to him. Joseph had saluted Him as *Rabboni Elias*. He was told that it was not Elijah, but Jesus: and the Lord at his request took him to the Sepulchre and shewed him the grave-clothes. 'Then I knew that it was Jesus, and I worshipped Him, and said, Blessed is He that cometh in the Name of the Lord.' They then went together to Arimathea, and he was bidden to abide there till the fortieth day. The Lord then said, 'I will go to My disciples,' and with these words He disappeared.

All this is taken almost word for word from the Latin version of the Gospel of Nicodemus[1]. But that book has no more to tell us of the story of Joseph of Arimathea.

Our writer now proceeds to say that Joseph became a disciple of Philip the apostle, who baptized him and his son Josephes. Afterwards he was appointed by St John to attend on the Blessed Virgin (in Jerusalem), while that apostle was busy at his work in Ephesus; and so it came about that he was present at her Assumption. The ground of this last statement would appear to be one of the Latin forms of the *Transitus Mariae*, or the

---

[1] Tischendorf, *Evangelia Apocrypha*, ed. 2, cc. 11, 12, and 15.

Passing of Mary, which claims to be written by Joseph of Arimathea himself[1].

The narrative then proceeds (p. 51):

In the fifteenth year after this he went to St Philip in Gaul, taking with him Josephes, whom the Lord had consecrated a bishop in the city of Sarath. For when the disciples were dispersed throughout the world after the Lord's Ascension Philip (as Freculfus tells us in the fourth chapter of his second book) went to the kingdom of the Franks, where he converted and baptized many. Then the apostle, desiring that the word of God should be spread abroad, sent twelve of his disciples to preach in Britain, placing at their head his favourite disciple Joseph of Arimathea, together with his son Josephes.

The last two sentences come from the thirteenth-century introduction prefixed to William of Malmesbury's book, save for the mention of Josephes in the final clause. What follows is a further extension of the story, and here the source of it is told us (p. 52):

There came with them (as it is read in the book which is called *The Holy Grail*) six hundred and more, both men and women, who all took a vow to abstain from matrimonial intercourse until they should have entered the land that was appointed for them. This vow all failed to keep, save one hundred and fifty; and these at the Lord's command crossed the sea on the shirt of Josephes on the night of the Lord's Resurrection, and reached land in the morning. When the rest repented and Josephes prayed for them, a ship was sent by the Lord, which King Solomon had curiously wrought in his day to last till the times of Christ. And so they reached their fellows on the same day.

We need not pursue in detail the story of their adventures. Joseph was imprisoned by the perfidious king

---

[1] Tischendorf, *Apocalypses Apocryphae*, pp. 113 ff.; MS C.

of North Wales. After his release by the king of Sarras, he and Josephes and ten others passed through Britain, where Arviragus was reigning, in the sixty-third year from the Incarnation of the Lord. This king, though he rejected their message, gave them the island of Yniswitrin, that is, the Glassy Isle. Here we are back again with the introduction prefixed to William of Malmesbury's book, save for the explanation of the name Yniswitrin. But four rude Latin verses follow, which introduce the name of Avalon.

> Avallon is entered by a band of Twelve:
> Joseph, Armathea's flower, is chief of them;
> And with his father cometh Josephes.
> So to these Twelve Glastonia's rights are given.

The lines are said to be by a certain metrical writer. The story of the building of the chapel follows as before. Joseph in due course is buried among his companions on the two-forked line next the oratory. The place became deserted and waste, until the Blessed Virgin chose that her oratory should once again be brought to the memory of the faithful.

Next follows (p. 55) the writing found in *The Deeds of King Arthur*, which we have already mentioned[1] as being one of the early marginal notes to the *De Antiquitate*.

Then comes over again the prophecy from the book of Melkin, as we have had it already, save that Melkin is here described as having been 'before Merlin.'

Presently (p. 56) a quotation is given us, from a source not mentioned, which traces the descent of King Arthur from the kindred of Joseph through his

[1] p. 29.

nephew Helaius. Another quotation declares that from Petrus, Joseph's cousin, was descended Loth, who married Arthur's sister, and whose sons were Walwan (i.e. Gawain) and three others.

Such is the lore of Glastonbury at the end of the fourteenth century concerning Joseph of Arimathea. We are now in a position to trace from the outset the successive stages of its development.

(1) Isidore of Seville († 638) says that St Philip preached Christ to the Gauls, and led the barbarous peoples, near neighbours of darkness and bordering on the tempestuous Ocean, to the light of knowledge and the harbour of faith.

(2) This is repeated (c. 830) by Freculfus, bishop of Lisieux (Bk. II, c. 4).

(3) The anonymous biographer of St Dunstan (writing c. 1000) records the legend that the first preachers of Christ in Britain found at Glastonbury a church built by no skill of man, and consecrated by our Lord Himself to the honour of His Virgin Mother.

(4) William of Malmesbury (c. 1130), though he knows this story, will not commit himself further than to say that, if St Philip preached in Gaul as Freculfus said, then it was not incredible that he should have sent disciples into Britain[1].

(5) The charter of St Patrick (c. 1220) marks a further development of the legend. The new points are

---

[1] It is important for the tracing of the growth of the legend to recall that between (4) and (5) the Great Fire of 1184 had intervened, followed as it was by the claim to the discovery of St Dunstan's remains and of King Arthur's body with the inscription which identified Glastonbury with Avalon (see above, pp. 12 ff.).

that we now have twelve disciples of St Philip and St James; that they build the church at the bidding of the archangel Gabriel; and that three pagan kings give them twelve portions of land.

(6) This is again developed shortly before 1250, by the final reviser of William of Malmesbury's book, in an introductory chapter which says that the leader of St Philip's disciples was Joseph of Arimathea, and that he arrived A.D. 63, in the fifteenth year after the Assumption of the Blessed Virgin.

(7) To this final edition of the *De Antiquitate* two marginal notes have been added, perhaps before the end of the thirteenth century. One tells us (p. 7) that Joseph was accompanied by his son Josephes and many others, and that he died on the island. The other (p. 45) gives the names of the three kings as Arviragus, Marius and Coillus, adding that the only son of the last of these was Lucius, the first Christian king of Britain. The former note mentions the Grail Legend as its source; the latter is derived from Geoffrey of Monmouth[1].

All this lay before John of Glastonbury, when at the end of the fourteenth century he recast the earlier history of the abbey. By him we are now given for the first time an orderly account of the full legend of Joseph of Arimathea as it was told at Glastonbury:

(1) The simplest form of St Joseph's early story— taken over word for word from the Gospel of Nicodemus.

(2) His attendance on the Blessed Virgin and his presence at her Assumption—from the *Transitus Mariae*.

---

[1] The further extension of the legend—'The Holy Thorn' and the Miracles (1502)—will come before us later.

(3) His connexion with St Philip who sends missionaries to Britain—an addition to the story which had been told in St Patrick's charter.

(4) The voyage to Britain on the miraculous shirt of his son Josephes; his imprisonment by the king of North Wales, and his release by King Mordrains—from 'the book which is called *The Holy Grail*.'

(5) His arrival at Glastonbury, his work and his burial there—Glastonbury additions to the legend of the Grail.

The most notable point about the Joseph story, as thus fully developed by the Glastonbury monks, is that, though confessedly based to a large extent on 'the book which is called *The Holy Grail*,' it knows nothing of the Grail itself.

The origin of the Grail legend, after all that has been written about it, remains obscure. But as the tales in connexion with which the Grail first makes its appearance are Celtic tales, it is now generally believed that the Grail itself has its prototypes in the mystic cauldron of unfailing supply and the magic cup of healing, which are also elements of Celtic mythology. When the Grail first appears in the romances it is as a marvellous vessel which passes round to feed the guests, or else as a cup which miraculously revives or heals. It is one of a group of talismans, which the hero must seek, and the meaning of which he must discover, as a condition of success. It is speedily Christianised and is linked with the name of Joseph of Arimathea, who is made to bring it to Britain. It is the Sacred Dish of the Last Supper in Jerusalem. Joseph had begged it of Pilate after the Lord's arrest. He had held it to catch the drops of the

Sacred Blood from the Cross. By an easy transition it becomes the Sacramental Cup of the Last Supper. Joseph was fed by it during the forty years of his imprisonment by the Jews, from which he was at last released by Vespasian. Joseph brought it with him on his travels, and when he came as the first Christian teacher to Britain it fed his hungering companions. It passed down in the line of his descendants who were kings or famous knights. Where was it? Who might see it? Then comes the search for it—the Quest of the Holy Grail. Arthur and his Round Table provide the heroes of this highest, holiest Quest.

Thus far Glastonbury has neither part nor lot in the matter. But the name of Avalon, already linked with Arthur, is occasionally mentioned or vaguely suggested in the Grail romances, though Joseph himself is not definitely brought thither. Joseph's part is played when he has accounted for the presence of the Grail in Britain. But Glastonbury, which at the beginning of the thirteenth century had claimed twelve disciples of St Philip as the first builders of its church of wattles, was ready by the middle of that century to place Joseph of Arimathea at their head, and to take over from the legend of the Grail the tale of his miraculous arrival in Britain.

But with the Grail itself Glastonbury would have nothing to do. It deliberately excised it from the story. It substituted the simpler version of Joseph's first imprisonment which it found in the Gospel of Nicodemus, in place of the later story of the imprisonment for forty years and the release by Vespasian[1], into which the

---

[1] As found in the *Vindicta Salvatoris* (Tischendorf, *Acta Apocrypha*, pp. 471 ff.)

romances had introduced the Grail as the means of his sustenance. It felt no qualms about accepting Josephes and his miraculous shirt, the persecution by the king of North Wales and the miraculous deliverance: but it left out all mention of the part played in these stories by the Grail. It even went so far as directly to exclude it by a counter-tradition, which declared that Joseph had brought two cruets filled with the blood and sweat of the Lord, and that these two cruets were buried with him in his grave.

All this is in harmony with the fact that the Holy Grail was purely an invention of the romances, and never at any time received ecclesiastical sanction. It was probably felt that the very conception was inconsistent with the reverence due to the Blessed Sacrament. Be that as it may, the fact remains that the Glastonbury tradition to the very end, though it borrowed what it wanted from 'the book which is called *The Holy Grail*,' makes no claim, no allusion even, to the Grail itself.

§ II. THE USE MADE OF THE TRADITION

At the risk of some repetition let us sum up the situation as we find it at the end of the fourteenth century. Glastonbury had by this time appropriated to itself the legend of St Joseph of Arimathea's mission to Britain, which had been evolved by the elaborators of the Grail romance as the means of accounting for the presence of that sacred vessel in this land. But, in taking over the legend from 'the book which is called *The Holy Grail*,' the Glastonbury chroniclers had made

certain significant alterations. They rejected that form
of the first part of Joseph's story which had been drawn
from the *Vindicta Salvatoris*, and which had made
Joseph a prisoner in Jerusalem for forty years, until his
ultimate release by Vespasian. This long imprisonment
had afforded to the romance writers an occasion for
introducing the Grail as the means by which Joseph
was miraculously fed. The Glastonbury writers substituted for this the more primitive legend found in the
Gospel of Nicodemus—a change which had the incidental advantage of enabling them to bring Joseph to
Glastonbury as early as the year 63. Moreover, though
they accepted Josephes and his miraculous shirt, and
certain other supernatural details, they everywhere
avoided all reference to the Grail. Indeed they put
forward a very different tradition, to the effect that
St Joseph had brought with him two silver cruets filled
with the blood and sweat of the Lord: and these two
cruets, it was affirmed, had been buried with him in his
grave. The story thus amended became such as might
readily receive ecclesiastical sanction, which never at
any time was given to the legend of the Holy Grail.

With the opening of the fifteenth century the practical
value of this appropriation of Joseph of Arimathea began
to appear. Not only did it enable the abbot of Glastonbury to press his claim to the first position among the
English abbots at a national synod, but it even acquired
international importance. It became a determining
factor when the precedence of the nations at a General
Council was in dispute. Archbishop Ussher has collected evidence of this for the Councils of Pisa in 1409,
Constance in 1417, Sienna in 1424; above all for the

PLATE IV

THE *MAGNA TABULA*

Council of Basle in 1434. When on this last occasion the Spaniards based their contention on the conversion of Spain by St James, the ancient books of Glastonbury were cited by the English in proof of their prior claim[1].

We now enter upon the last hundred years of the abbey's history. The legend of its founder had by this time reached its full maturity. Hardly anything was added to it as long as the abbey stood. All that remained was to impress it on the imagination of successive generations of reverential pilgrims; and this was attempted in more ways than one.

(1) Ussher makes frequent quotations from what he calls the *Magna Tabula* of Glastonbury[2]. He speaks of it as in the possession of Lord William Howard, the son of Thomas, duke of Norfolk. This Howard is the 'Belted Will' of the *Lay of the Last Minstrel*. He restored Naworth Castle in Cumberland, and collected there many valuable books and manuscripts. In 1887 Mr J. A. Bennett, F.S.A., rector of South Cadbury, visited Naworth Castle in order to examine this *Tabula*, and he has given a full description of it, together with a photograph, in the *Somerset Archaeological Society's Proceedings* (XXXIV, 117 ff.):

It was a folding wooden frame, 3 ft. 8 in. in height, and 3 ft. 6 in. in breadth when opened flat, containing two wooden leaves somewhat smaller, so that they may fold within the outer case when closed, like the pages of a book. All the six interior faces are covered with MS written upon

---

[1] *Britannicarum Ecclesiarum Antiquitates*, c. ii. At Pisa and Constance the French had countered the English claim by the tradition of the preaching of Mary Magdalen, Martha and Lazarus in Provence: Hefele, *Councils* (ed. Leclercq, 1916), VII, pt. i, p. 31 *n*.

[2] Ussher, l.c.

parchment affixed to the surface of the wood. There are
three pairs of nail holes in the upper, and four pairs in the
lower edges of the frame, upon the left hand only. These
seem to show that it was affixed to a wall in such a way that
it might be opened out as a book. The whole MS takes up
about sixty pages, clearly written, of ordinary exercise book
size.

From the table of contents which Mr Bennett has drawn
up it would appear that the whole is copied from John
of Glastonbury's *History*, with the exception of the
closing section, which is new, and is headed: 'Of the
Chapel of Saints Michael and Joseph, and all saints
who rest in the cemetery.' This chapel, we are told, was
in the midst of the cemetery: it had fallen into disrepair
and was restored by Abbot John Chinnock in 1382. The
abbot had three images made—of Joseph, of Nicodemus, and of our Lord being taken down from the Cross:
the middle figure, that of our Lord, was of the stature
which the Glastonbury tradition declared to be that of
the Sacred Body itself. This seems to be the earliest
mention of St Joseph's name in any connexion with a
chapel.

The *Tabula* was probably set up in a conspicuous
place in the church for the edification of visitors. It
told in full the stories of Joseph of Arimathea and of
King Arthur, of St Patrick and his charter, of the translation of the body of St Dunstan, and much besides.

(2) This was not the only means by which the attention of pilgrims was directed to St Joseph of Arimathea
and the church which he had built. To the north of the
Lady Chapel stood a column, which is sometimes called
a pyramid and sometimes a cross. The circular founda-

PLATE V

Anno poſt paſſione do-
mini xxxi· duodecī ſcī ex quibʒ
Joſeph ab arimathia priuſ erat huc
uenerūt· qui ecciam huj regni prima in hoc
loco coſtruxerūt· qui xpͤ i honoꝛ ſue mͥris ⁊ locī p
eoꝝ ſepultura pſencialit̾ dedicauit· ſcͦ dauid mene
uecͥū archiepͦ hoc teſtante· Qui dns̄ ecciam illā dedicͤ
re diſponͤti in ſopͥnis· apͥaruit ⁊ eū a propoſito reuo
cauit· necnͦ i ſignū qd͛ ipͤ dns̄ ecciam ipam priuſ cū
cimiterio dedicauat· manͥ epi digitͦ ꝑforauit ⁊ ſic ꝑ
forata mltis uidētibʒ i craſtio apͥaruit· poſtea uͦ ide͂
epͥc dͦno reuelate· ac ſcoꝛ͂ numͥo in eade creſcēte· quēdā
cancellū i orientali parte huic eccie adiecit ⁊ i honore
eate uirginis coſecrauit· Cui altaꝛ̄ ieſtimabili
ſaphiro i ꝑꝑetuā huj rei memͥriā inſignuūt·
Et ne loc̾ aut qntitas porͣˢ eccie
ꝑ tales augmͤtacͦes obli
uiͦni tradeꝛ· erigit̾·

/hͥc columͥna illineͣ ꝑ·
duoſ orientales angulos·
eiuſdͥ eccie uſ͛ meridiem ꝑ
tracta ⁊ pͥdictū cancellū ab ea obuiͣˢ·
eunte· Et erat eͥ longitudo ab illa linea uſ͛ oc
cidentͤ· lx· pedū· latitudo uͦ eͥ· xxvi· pedum·
diſtancͣa centri iſti columͥne a puncto me
dio iꝑ poſitos angulos· xlviij· pͤdum·

PLATE FROM COLUMN NORTH OF LADY CHAPEL

tions of the base of this column, about seven feet in diameter, were uncovered in 1921[1]. It was erected in order to indicate the exact site of the earliest church; and it bore a brass plate, the existence of which can be traced as late as the second quarter of the seventeenth century[2]. The inscription on this plate, of which a facsimile is given in the first volume of Spelman's *Concilia*, relates in brief the coming of Joseph of Arimathea and the dedication by our Lord Himself of the church built in honour of His Virgin Mother; the vision of St David, the chapel or chancel added by him, and the gift of his famous sapphire. It then proceeds as follows:

And lest the site or size of the earlier church should come to be forgotten by reason of such additions, this pillar is erected on a line extended southward through the two eastern angles of the same church, and cutting off from it the chancel aforesaid. And its length was 60 feet westward from that line; its width 26 feet; the distance of the centre of this pillar from the middle point between the said angles 48 feet.

These indications mark, as a matter of fact, the site and extent of the Lady Chapel which was built immediately after the Great Fire of 1184. This chapel had however been enlarged in later days: for the Galilee had been built at its east end, to link it on to the Great Church, and the Lady Chapel had then been extended by the removal of its eastern wall. The assumption was—absurd as it may seem to us—that the Lady Chapel as built after the fire not only occupied the site of the earliest church, but covered exactly the same area. The column therefore was erected outside, in the line of

[1] See Additional Note II.   [2] See Additional Note III.

junction between the Lady Chapel proper and the
Galilee which formed its extension, in order to mark
the original eastern limit. Its inscription encouraged
the intelligent visitor to gaze with reverential awe on
this most sacred spot, and to recall the amazing story
of the past[1].

(3) It is not until the closing years of the abbey's
history that we learn that St Joseph worked miracles of
healing. In 1502, or shortly afterwards, a poem was
written under the title of *The Lyfe of Joseph of Armathia.*
It was printed by Pynson in 1520, and re-printed from
him by Skeat in 1871[2]. The poem is based mainly on
John of Glastonbury's narrative, and it is only the
additional details that are of interest to us here. A few
stanzas may be quoted:

> But yet whan Ioseph Ihesu downe toke,
> The syde that the wound was on lay to his brest;
> The colde blode that was at our lordes herte rote
> Fell within Iosephes sherte and lay on his chest;
> Truly as holy scripture sayth there did it rest
> At the holy place aboue his stomake,
> And when our lorde in the sendony was drest,
> This blode in two cruettes Ioseph did take.

The two cruets are figured in a heraldic shield, which is
reproduced from Pynson in Skeat's edition. Of this
shield we shall hear further presently. After Joseph
had been instructed to build a chapel 'of our ladyes
assumption,' we read:

> So Ioseph dyd as the aungell hym bad,
> And wrought there an ymage of our lady;
> For to serue hyr great deuocion he had;

---

[1] See Additional Note III.
[2] Early English Text Soc. vol. 44, pp. 37–52.

And that same ymage is yet at Glastenbury,
In the same church; there ye may it se.
For it was the fyrst, as I understande,
That euer was sene in this countre;
For Ioseph it made wyth his owne hande.

The next stanza begins: 'The rode of northdore of
London also dyd he make.' Skeat quotes a reference
to this Rood as an object of pilgrimage from Pecock's
Repressor (ed. C. Babington, I, 194).

Presently a series of miraculous cures wrought by
St Joseph is recorded at full length. The sick folk come
from Wells, Doulting, Banwell, Ilchester, Yeovil,
Milborne Port, Compton, Pilton. Towards the end we
read:

Great meruaylles men may se at Glastenbury;
One of the walnot tree that there dooth stande,
In the holy grounde called the semetory,
Harde by the place where kynge Arthur was founde;
South fro Iosephs chapell it is walled in rounde;
It bereth no leaues tyll the day of saint Barnabè;
And than that tree, that standeth in the grounde,
Spredeth his leaues as fayre as any other tree.

Here we have what seems to be the first instance of
the name of St Joseph's Chapel being applied to the
western Lady Chapel or any part of it.

Thre hawthornes also, that groweth in Werall,
Do burge and bere grene leaues at Christmas
As freshe as other in May...

This is the first mention of the Holy Thorn: the legend
that it sprang from Joseph's staff, when he rested with
his company on 'Weary-all' hill, had apparently not
yet made its appearance.

A last fleeting glimpse at medieval Glastonbury is
given us in a page of reminiscences by one who as a boy
had served Mass at St Joseph's altar there. William
Good was born at Glastonbury in 1527. He went up to
Oxford, and was a scholar and afterwards a fellow of
Corpus Christi College. For a brief period under
Queen Mary he was rector of Middle Chinnock in
Somerset, and prebendary of Combe VIII in the
cathedral church of Wells. He was afterwards a
member of the Society of Jesus, and died at Naples
in 1586. These facts are taken by permission from an
article in the *Downside Review* for March 1897 by Dom
Gasquet (now Cardinal Gasquet), who translated the
passage which here follows from a manuscript in the
English College at Rome[1].

At Glastonbury there were bronze plates as a perpetual
memorial, chapels, crypts, crosses, arms, the keeping of the
feast (of St Joseph) on July 27th, as long as the monks
enjoyed the protection of kings by their charters. Now all
these things have perished in the ruins. The monks never
knew for certain the place of this saint's burial, or pointed
it out. They said the body was hidden most carefully, either
there (at Glastonbury), or on a hill near Montacute, called
Hamden Hill, and that when his body should be found, the
whole world should wend their way thither on account of
the number and wondrous nature of the miracles worked
there.

Amongst other things, I remember to have seen at Glastonbury on a stone cross, overthrown during this Queen's
reign, a bronze plate, on which was carved an inscription
relating that Joseph of Arimathea came to Britain thirty
years after Christ's Passion, with eleven or twelve com-

---

[1] See Additional Note VI.

panions: that he was allowed by Arviragus the king to dwell at Glastonbury, which was then an island called Avalon, in a simple and solitary life: and that he had brought with him two small silver vessels in which was some of the most holy blood and water which had flowed from the side of the dead Christ.

This cross, moreover, had been set up many years before to mark the length of the chapel to the Blessed Virgin, made by St Joseph with hurdles. The length was measured by a straight line from the centre of the cross to the side of the chancel afterwards built of hewn stone, under which also there was of old, in a subterranean crypt, the Chapel of St Joseph. Outside, in the wall of this Chapel of the Blessed Virgin, there was a stone with the words *Jesus*, *Maria*, carved in very ancient letters. The old arms of the Monastery of Glastonbury confirm (the traditions). These arms are a white shield on which is placed vertically the stem of a green[1] cross, and from side to side the arms of a cross in like manner. Drops of blood are scattered over the field of the shield; on both sides of the upright and under the arms of the cross are set golden *ampullae*. These were always called St Joseph's insignia, for he was piously believed to have lived there; and even perhaps to have been buried there.

There was likewise at Glastonbury, in a long subterranean chapel, a most famous place of pilgrimage, which was made to a stone image of the saint there, and many miracles were wrought at it. When I was a boy of eight, for I was born there, I have served Mass in this chapel, and I saw it destroyed in the time of Henry VIII by a wicked man, one William Goals.

The first point of interest here to be noted is the uncertainty which to the end prevailed as to the burial place

[1] The Latin adds *et nodosae* (i.e. 'raguly'): see Additional Note VI.

of Joseph of Arimathea. The prophecy of Melkin had
said that he was buried 'on a two-forked line' (*in linea
bifurcata*), whatever that might mean. After the column
had been erected on the north side of the Lady
Chapel, it had been suggested that this was the line
spoken of in the inscription on the brass plate[1]. On
10 June 1345 a certain J. Blome had obtained a royal
writ authorising him to make search at Glastonbury,
if the abbot should permit, for the body of Joseph
of Arimathea; but we are not told the result of this
enquiry[2]. It is certainly strange to learn from William
Good's account that the monks after all were not
sure whether the body lay within their own precincts
or not.

Secondly, we get here the explanation of the later
confusion by which the name of St Joseph's Chapel
came to be applied to the Lady Chapel. Whether, as
seems to be suggested, St Joseph's Chapel was in a
crypt before the large crypt under the Lady Chapel was
made, may be left for the present undetermined; but it
is plain that this later crypt was the place of pilgrimage
frequented by those who sought for healing through
St Joseph's intercession. It is also worth while to note
that the cures were associated with the image of the
saint, and not with any sacred well. It does not appear that healing power was supposed to attach to
any spring at Glastonbury before the middle of the
eighteenth century.

Lastly, we may note that the words JESUS MARIA are
still to be seen on the outside of the south wall of the

---

[1] See Additional Note II.
[2] See Additional Note IV.

PLATE VI

ON SOUTH WALL OF LADY CHAPEL

Lady Chapel[1]: and that the arms of St Joseph, the green cross raguly with the blood-drops and the two cruets, are figured in what is said to be sixteenth-century glass in the south window of the chancel of the parish church of St John[2]. A sketch of them may be seen in the *Somerset Year Book* for 1924 (p. 75).

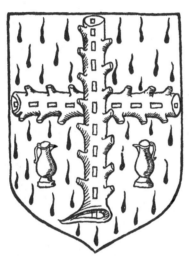

Arms of St Joseph of Arimathea

The legends which we have been considering are not sacred in the religious sense, but they are truly venerable traditions which greatly influenced the story of the past and have left an abiding mark on the nomenclature

---

[1] In this connexion it is of interest to note that in the time of Abbot Adam of Sodbury (1322–34) Master Edmund Stourton, a learned monk of the abbey, wrote a book entitled *De nominibus Ihesu et Mariae* (*John of Glast.* p. 47).

[2] For other examples see Additional Note V.

of the present. They are not very ancient, when the long life of the abbey is taken into account. From first to last they occupied only the last three centuries and a half of its history. They were unknown to William of Malmesbury when he wrote his book, *On the Antiquity of the Church of Glastonbury*, about the year 1125, although he had free access to all the abbey's records before the Great Fire and made, as we now know, excellent use of his opportunities of investigation. Our earliest date for any of them is 1191. Yet they claim respectful treatment on very various grounds. He who rejects them as unworthy trivialities, and will have nothing but the unclothed skeleton of historically attested fact, cuts out the poetry from life, and renders himself incapable of understanding the fulness of his inheritance. Even the severe historian may not neglect the beliefs and fancies which have come to weave themselves about a people's daily life: their very vogue has become a fact of history itself. Still less can the student of medieval literature afford to miss the lesson here presented to us of the progressive modification of great popular themes, long after they have ceased to be subject to the vicissitudes of merely oral transmission and have been enshrined in famous writings—a modification due to the instinct of appropriation and the desire to give them local colour.

ADDITIONAL NOTES

I

The Expected Return of King Arthur

1. The belief that Arthur would some day come again was not extinguished, even at Glastonbury itself, by the discovery of his tomb. 'The common tradition,' Collinson says (II, 240), 'was that he suffered only a temporary kind of death, and that he would come again to reassume the sceptre.' He goes on to quote lines from a poem on Arthur in the Marquis of Bath's MS entitled *Liber Rubeus Bathoniae* (A.D. 1428), which has been edited by Dr Furnivall for the Early English Text Society (vol. 2):

> But for he skaped that batell y-wys,
> Bretons and Cornysch seyeth thus,
> That he levyth yut, pardé,
> And schall come and be a kyng aye.

> At Glastynbury on the queer,
> They made Artourez toumbe there,
> And wrote with latyn vers thus
> *Hic jacet Arthurus, rex quondam, rexque futurus.*

2. A remarkable illustration of what William of Malmesbury calls 'the idle tales of the Britons' regarding the survival of King Arthur comes to us from a French writer of the first half of the twelfth century. In 1112 the city of Laon was burnt in a popular insurrection against the bishop. The clerks of the cathedral church set out on a pilgrimage with the shrine of the Blessed Virgin to collect money for rebuilding. In the following year they extended their pilgrimage across the Channel, and visited Canterbury and many other places in the south of England. Everywhere their visits were marked by miracles of healing and other supernatural occurrences. They passed through Winchester and Christchurch in Hampshire to Exeter: thence they were led to retrace their steps to Salisbury. After visiting the abbey

of Wilton, which claimed to have the tomb of the Venerable
Bede at which cures were not infrequent, they returned to
Exeter. At this point the narrative runs as follows:

> Thence we came into the province called Danavexeria,
> where they shewed us the Seat and the Oven (*cathedram et
> furnum*) of that King Arthur, who is famous in the tales of the
> Britons. There we were highly honoured by a clerk named
> Algardus, who had stayed a long while in Laon, and who after-
> wards became bishop of Coutances in Normandy. [A blind
> girl and a deaf boy were healed at Bodmin.] Moreover a
> man there with a withered hand was keeping vigil before the
> shrine for his healing. But, just as the Bretons quarrel with
> the Frenchmen about King Arthur, so this man began to
> contend with one of our attendants named Haganel, who
> belonged to the household of Guy the archdeacon of Laon,
> saying that Arthur was still alive. Whence no small tumult
> arose, many rushed into the church with arms, and unless the
> aforesaid clerk Algardus had intervened the matter would
> have almost come to the shedding of blood. Such a quarrel
> before her shrine was, we believe, displeasing to Our Lady:
> for the man with the withered hand, who had caused the
> tumult about Arthur, got no cure. (Hermannus, *De mirac. S.
> Mariae Laudun*, II, 15: *P.L.* 156, 983.)

Though this narrative is told in the first person, its writer
was not one of those who came to England with the party;
but a monk named Hermann, who composed three books,
On the Miracles of St Mary of Laon, in the name of the
canons of Laon, and dedicated the work to Bartholomew
who was bishop from 1113 to 1151. We may readily accept
what he says of the opinion of the Cornish folk about King
Arthur in the year 1113.

3. Whatever the monks of Glastonbury might say as to
their possession of King Arthur's grave, they failed to
convince the peasants of South Cadbury, a dozen miles
away, that he and his knights were not sleeping under the
great hill known as Cadbury Castle. Leland found this
belief current about 1540, and it is attested continuously

down to our own times. A summary of notices regarding it will be seen in the *Somerset Archaeological Society's Proceedings*, LIX, ii, 3 ff. To these I may add the following, sent me recently by a friend:

'When I was a student at Wells Theological College in the year 1902, the late Mr A. Clarke, an old artist and antiquarian who was then living in the Vicars' Close, told me that he had paid a visit with a party of antiquaries to Cadbury Camp, and while there, had been approached by an old man, a native of the place, with the question, *Have you come to take the king out?*'

II

The 'Old Church' at Glastonbury

Our principal authority for the early history of Glastonbury is William of Malmesbury's book, *On the Antiquity of the Church of Glastonbury*. Unfortunately the book has not come down to us in its original form. The edition of Hearne from the MS at Trinity College, Cambridge (in the first volume of his *Adam of Domerham*), shows that the *De Antiquitate* as there presented is full of interpolations made a century or so after the author's death. Happily however a large part of the beginning of the work was embodied by William of Malmesbury himself in the so-called third edition of his *Gesta Regum* which he issued about 1140, that is, soon after he had completed the *De Antiquitate*. For the passages thus quoted we are on solid ground: they will be referred to hereafter as $G.R._3$ with the pages of the Rolls Series edition.

The evidence of William of Malmesbury, where we are certain that we have his own words, is of special value, as it gives us the result of personal observations or the record of tradition previous to the great fire of 1184. Immediately after the fire legend broke out in extravagant forms, and the *De Antiquitate* was recast and interpolated in order to accommodate it to the beliefs which had come to find acceptance.

Of the earliest church at Glastonbury William of Malmesbury speaks with great caution. If it was true, he says, that St Philip preached in Gaul, it was not incredible that he should have sent disciples to preach in Britain. The first statement of real interest that he makes is that it was said by the tradition of the seniors that Paulinus, who became bishop of Rochester after fleeing from York, had covered the wattled church with wooden boarding (*ligneo tabulatu*). These are certainly William of Malmesbury's own words (*De Antiq.* p. 28, attested by *G.R.*₃, p. 28); but what follows in the *De Antiquitate* may possibly be a later addition; it is to the effect that he also covered it from top to bottom with lead[1]. We may fairly assume that in William of Malmesbury's time the wattled church presented an appearance which corresponded in some way to this tradition.

After telling of St David's vision, which led him to refrain from consecrating the Old Church (*vetusta ecclesia*), he says that the saint speedily built another church and consecrated that (*De Antiq.* p. 26, *G.R.*₃, p. 28).

Then in *G.R.*₃, p. 36, he says that King Ina built from the foundations the church of the blessed Apostles, as an appendix to the Old Church. In the *De Antiq.* (p. 53) we read that he 'founded the greater church of the Apostles Peter and Paul; and inasmuch as there have been several basilicas there,' it is well to describe them. But these words and the fanciful description which follows are the composition of a later writer. King Ina's great church itself is a certainty—we find it mentioned in a tenth-century Saxon genealogy[2].

---

[1] An interesting parallel to this use of lead is found in Bede, *H.E.* III, 25. Finan, who succeeded Aidan at Lindisfarne in 651, built a new church wholly of timber, and roofed it with reeds. Eadberct, who followed St Cuthbert in 687, took off the reeds and covered the whole, roof and walls alike, with lead.

[2] Cotton MS, *Tib.* B. 5, f. 23.

That the Old Church perished in the fire of 1184 we gather from Adam of Domerham (p. 335): Ralph fitz Stephen[1] 'built the church of St Mary in the place where originally the Old Church had stood'; and he proceeds to speak of bones dug up at that time *in vetusta ecclesia*. John of Glastonbury (p. 89), after giving the story of St Paulinus from the *De Antiquitate*, adds: 'And so that holy oratory in the same fashion remained until the burning of the church.'

On the other hand, King Ina's church had disappeared. The *De Antiquitate* (p. 117) tells us that Abbot Herlwin [1101-1120], considering that the church begun by his immediate predecessor did not correspond with the wealth and dignity of the abbey, pulled it down and began a new one, on which he expended 480 pounds. As Henry of Blois, though he built much at Glastonbury, is never said to have built any part of the church, we must conclude that it had been completed before 1125.

These facts are recognised by Professor Willis in his *Architectural History of Glastonbury Abbey*, published in 1866. This remarkable man was the first to make a scientific study of ancient buildings in the light thrown upon them by their recorded history and traditions. He combined minute accuracy of observation and measurement with a patient research which collected and sifted the documentary evidence. With his architectural judgments marvellously little fault has been found by qualified investigators. If his interpretation of the documentary evidence is sometimes open to criticism, this is no more than might be expected in the case of one who broke so much new ground. He has at any rate the merit of supplying by his quotations or references the means of testing and, if need be, correcting the statements which he makes.

---

[1] He was not, as has been sometimes stated, the son of King Stephen, but of Stephen the king's chamberlain. He acted as the king's business man in the building of Witham Charterhouse and in the re-building of Glastonbury. We learn this from the Pipe Rolls.

This much of apology is needed before I venture to call attention to a curious error which seems hitherto to have escaped notice. In the plan of the abbey prefixed to his book he has indicated by the letter *k* a point on the south side of the Lady Chapel, at which, as he explains on pp. 19 f., he would locate a certain pillar in the monks' cemetery, set up to preserve the recollection of the site and size of the Old Church.

The documents which supply the evidence for this are two. One is a brass plate, dug up at Glastonbury and now apparently lost, of which an exact representation is given by Spelman in the first volume of his *Concilia* (1639). After recounting the coming of Joseph of Arimathea and the dedication of the first church to the Virgin by the Saviour Himself, it mentions St David's vision and his addition of a kind of chancel to the primitive church (*quemdam cancellum in orientali parte huic ecclesiæ adjecit*): this he consecrated to the Virgin, adorning its altar with his famous sapphire. It then proceeds to give this account of the pillar to which it was fixed:

Et ne locus aut quantitas prioris ecclesie per tales augmentaciones oblivioni traderetur, erigitur hec columpna in linea per duos orientales angulos ejusdem ecclesie versus meridiem protracta, et predictum cancellum ab ea abscindente. Et erat ejus longitudo ab illa linea versus occidentem lx pedum, latitudo vero ejus xxvi pedum, distancia centri istius columpne a puncto medio inter predictos angulos xlviii pedum.

I take this to mean that the pillar stood outside on the north. A straight line drawn from its centre southward through the two eastern corners of the Lady Chapel would mark the division between the primitive church and the addition made to it by St David. I therefore translate as follows:

And lest the site or size of the earlier church should come to be forgotten by reason of such additions, this pillar is erected on a line extended southward through the two eastern angles of the same church, and cutting off from it the chancel aforesaid. And its length was 60 feet westward from that line; its width 26 feet; the distance of the centre of this pillar from the middle point between the said angles 48 feet.

Professor Willis, however, translated the crucial words thus: 'This column was erected on a line passing through the two eastern angles of that church, and protracted southward, thus cutting off the aforesaid chancel.' It will be observed that he had taken away the word *et*, which follows *protracta*, and placed it before *versus meridiem*: he supplies the word 'thus' to introduce the final clause. He accordingly interprets the passage to mean that the pillar was on the *south* side of the Lady Chapel!

Now let us turn to the other document. It is printed by Hearne immediately before the prologue of John of Glastonbury's *History*, with which it has no kind of connexion. It is also printed, without the last sentences, in the original edition of the *Monasticon Anglicanum* (I. 1.), though not by the later editors: here it is said to be taken from a Cotton MS. It is in fact a Church lection, ending with versicle and response, and followed by the prose and collect for the Mass of St Joseph of Arimathea's Day. It is a late compilation from various sources, most of which we can trace, giving an outline of the traditional history of the Old Church. The passage with which we are concerned is quoted in the original Latin by Willis in a footnote to p. 20: his translation of it follows on p. 21. Here we have again the story of St David, and the statement that 'he added to this church another and smaller chapel, after the manner of a chancel, on the east'—words partly identical with those of the brass plate. It then proceeds:

Et ut semper nosceretur ubi capellae istae conjungebantur, quaedam piramis in parte septemtrionali exterius et quidam gradus interius et meridies linialiter eas abscindunt. Juxta quam lineam, secundum quosdam antiquorum, jacet sanctus Joseph cum magna multitudine sanctorum.

Professor Willis renders this by the following paraphrase:

And that the point where this chancel joined the church might be always known, a certain pyramid outside on the south, and a certain interior step within, on the same meridian line, marked the division between them. Near this line, according to certain ancient writers, lies St Joseph with a great multitude of saints.

We may accept this with the omission of the word 'interior' before 'step,' and with the more serious change of 'south' into 'north.' We can but suppose that the professor had so fully convinced himself from his study of the inscription on the brass plate that the pillar was on the south side, that he inadvertently rendered *septemtrionali* as 'south.'

This liturgical piece gives us no fresh evidence, except as to the step up into the chancel: its compiler has embodied much of the language of the inscribed plate; he must have seen it in position, and we cannot reject his testimony as to the side of the Lady Chapel on which it stood.

[The substance of this Note appeared in *Som. and Dors. Notes and Queries*, XVII, 58 (Aug. 1921). Soon after it was written the ground was opened at the point indicated on the north side of the Lady Chapel, and the foundation was uncovered of the base of the column, a circle of about seven feet in diameter.]

III

1. *The Leaden Cross from King Arthur's Grave*

Camden in his *Britannia* (p. 166 of ed. 1607) writes: 'Inscriptionem autem ex Protypo in Glasconiensi cœnobio quondam descriptam propter literarum antiquitatem subiungendam putavi.' The Cross, as it is shewn in our illustration, appears for the first time in this edition. In previous editions no cross is figured, but only the antique letters, which are arranged thus:

HIC IACET SEP-
VLTVS INCLITVS
REX ARTVRIVS IN
INSVLA AVALO
NIA

In Gibson's edition (1695) the block with the Cross of 1607 has been copied with minute variations.

The form of the Cross, and the arrangement of the letters upon it, would seem to have been an after-thought on Camden's part: it is only the antique form of the letters for which he expressly vouches.

Sharon Turner in his *History of the Anglo-Saxons*, I, 276, *n.* 43 of ed. 3 (I, 293, *n.* 45 of ed. 6), says: 'A facsimile of this inscription is given in Gibson's *Camden*, p. 66; and in Whitaker's *Manchester*, part ii. Dr Whitaker was told that the cross had then lately been in the possession of Mr Chancellor Hughes, at Wells.' In this eccentric *History of Manchester*, published in 1771 and 1775, the Cross is figured after Gibson's *Camden* (1695); but I have failed to find any reference to Chancellor Hughes in the book. Sharon Turner may have had the information directly from Whitaker.

2. *The Brass Plate from the Column*

Bishop Godwin in his *Catalogue of the Bishops of England* (ed. 1615, p. 11) speaks of this plate as 'remaining in the custody of Th. Hughes, of Welles, Esqvier,' and says that he himself had lately read it. Sir Henry Spelman (1639) says that it came into the hands of Sir Thomas Hughes ('D. Thomæ Hugonis, Eq. aur.'); and it was by favour of his son that he was enabled to present a facsimile from the brass itself. In Warner's *Glastonbury* (App. p. xxxix) we read in a footnote: 'This inscription was in brass, and in Mr Broughton's time, or a little before, in the custody of Thomas Hewes, of the city of Wells, esquire—Broughton, Age I, cap. 22, page 110.' Richard Broughton died 1634.

The Hewes family seems to have been of long standing

in Wells: a lease of a tenement to Edith Hewes widow in
1502 is among the charters of the dean and chapter, and the
burial of Dr Hewes is recorded in 1587–8. (*Cal. of Wells
MSS*, II, 312, 697). It is not unlikely that William Hughes,
chancellor of the diocese († 1716), whose son was city clerk,
was of the same family (Jewers, *Wells Monuments*, pp. 63 f.).
It was in the possession of Chancellor Hughes, as we have
seen, that the cross from King Arthur's grave was said
to have been. It is of interest to add that he gave a copy of
Spelman's *Concilia* to the Chapter Library.

IV

The Grave of St Joseph of Arimathea

We have ventured above (p. 30) to give a free rendering
of the untranslateable words of Melkin's prophecy: the
Latin is so curious that it must be given in full. John of
Glastonbury has it twice over, on p. 30 and again on p. 55.

Insula Avallonis avida funere paganorum, præ ceteris in
orbe ad sepulturam eorum omnium sperulis propheciæ
vaticinantibus decorata, et in futurum ornata erit altissimum
laudantibus. *Abbadare*, potens in *Saphat*, paganorum nobilis-
simus, cum centum quatuor milibus dormicionem ibi accepit.
Inter quos Joseph de marmore, ab Arimathia nomine, cepit
sompnum perpetuum; et jacet in linea bifurcata, juxta
meridianum angulum oratorii, cratibus præparatis [*lege* -ti],
super potentem adorandam virginem, supradictis sperulatis
locum habitantibus tredecim. Habet enim secum Joseph in
sarcophago duo fassula alba et argentea, cruore prophetæ
Ihesu et sudore perimpleta. Cum reperietur ejus sarcopha-
gum integrum illibatum, in futuris videbitur, et erit apertum
toto orbi terrarum. Extunc nec aqua, nec ros cœli, insulam
nobilissimam habitantibus poterit deficere. Per multum
tempus ante diem judicialem in Iosaphat erunt aperta hæc,
et viventibus declarata.

At the meaning of some of these words I have only been
able to guess. Thus I have imagined that *sperulis* may have

been mis-written for *spherulis*, a diminutive of *sphera* in an astronomical sense. Similarly I have taken *sperulatis* as possibly meaning 'pointed to by the prophesying spheres'; but I feel no confidence in these suggestions[1].

Again, *Joseph de marmore, ab Arimathia nomine*, may suggest a marble tomb or a stone coffin. What else can the meaning be?

But the puzzle of the piece is the statement that St Joseph was buried *in linea bifurcata*. The phrase seized on the imagination, and it was repeated by various writers. I have given it the most obvious rendering, 'on a two-forked line,' which might mean, for instance, 'where a path divides.' But Professor Willis in his *Architectural History of Glastonbury Abbey* (p. 16 *n*.) gives it quite a different interpretation:

> *Linea*, according to Ducange, is an under garment, close fitting, and made of linen...'*a camisia, subucula*, or shirt.' The epithet *bifurcata*, peculiar, I believe, to this example, appears to imply that it was divided below into two flaps like that ordinary garment. The passage therefore simply reads that Joseph of Arimathea was buried in a linen shirt. A *dalmatic*, being open at the sides below, also deserves the epithet bifurcate.

On this some remarks must be made. It is true that *linea* is used for a shirt: indeed it is actually contrasted with a dalmatic in a passage quoted by Ducange from the Passion of St Cyprian: 'After he had stripped himself of his *dalmatica* and handed it over to the deacons, he stood *in linea* awaiting the executioner.' It is then quite conceivable that Joseph of Arimathea should have been buried in his shirt. Indeed a shirt plays a part in his legend at an early point.

The English poem from which we have quoted above

---

[1] Dom Chapman has since informed me that *sperula* is the spelling of many MSS of the Vulgate in Exod. xxv and xxxvii (in xxxvii, 22 the best MSS have *sphaerae*, and there only). The Hebrew word is rendered 'knop' in A.V.; and a small ball-ornament seems to be intended.

(p. 44) has the strange statement that at the Burying of the Lord His cold blood

> Fell within Iosephes sherte and lay on his chest,

and that it was this blood that was preserved in the 'two cruettes.' The shirt therefore might well have served as the vesture of St Joseph's own burial, even as the two cruets were laid at his side.

But what can be the meaning of a 'bifurcate' or 'two-forked' shirt? The word *bifurcatus* is not so uncommon as Professor Willis supposed. The classical form of the adjective indeed is *bifurcus*: but Ducange quotes the verb of which *bifurcatus* is the participle from a charter of 1222: 'prope locum ubi illa semita bifurcatur'; and the fork of a path is an expression intelligible enough.

A more difficult use of the word occurs in Thorne's *History of St Augustine's, Canterbury* (Twysden, *Decem Scriptores*, col. 1763, l. 41), where among the relics given by St Augustine to his abbey he mentions *crux bifurcata*, 'a two-forked cross.' Thorne had evidently taken over the term from an earlier writer, Thomas Sprot, whose work has not survived. For Elmham, the later chronicler of the abbey, being clearly puzzled by it, describes the cross as 'two-fold or duplicated (*geminata sive duplicata*), which by Thomas Sprot and other writers is called *bifurcata*.'

I may add, from the Supplement to Ducange, that Wyclif spoke of 'bifurcate canons' (*bifurcati canonici*), playing on the shape of their caps (*in Trialogo*, art. 10).

But these examples do not help us to the meaning of the epithet as applied to the shirt.

We have however to face the fact that some of the writers of a later time understood *in linea bifurcata* as an indication of locality, 'on the two-forked line.' This is probably implied in its incidental mention by William of Worcester, who measured and described the abbey church about the year 1478 (Willis, *ut supra*, p. 17):

And opposite the second window [of the Lady Chapel]

on the south there are in the cemetery two stone crosses hollowed, where the bones of King Arthur were buried, where *in linea bifurcata* lies Joseph of Arimathea.

It undoubtedly was so understood by the writer of the late liturgical piece prefixed by Hearne to John of Glastonbury's *History* (see Additional Note II). After speaking of *the line* from the pillar outside on the north through the point up to which the eastern end of the Old Church originally came, he says: '*Near this line*, according to certain ancient writers, lies St Joseph with a great multitude of saints.' And it may seem as if John of Glastonbury himself had taken the local view; for he says (p. 54): 'Amongst whom Joseph also was buried and placed (*et positus*) *in linea bifurcata* over against the aforesaid oratory.'

I have therefore given the rendering 'on a two-forked line,' as this interpretation has at any rate some medieval precedent. But it must be admitted that the words are as ambiguous as those of a Delphic oracle.

We have lastly to consider what was the prevailing view at Glastonbury itself as to the serious question whether Joseph of Arimathea was buried there or not. It is plain from passages which we have cited that John of Glastonbury believed that he was; and William of Worcester found the same belief current towards the end of the fifteenth century. The writer of the late liturgical piece does not quite definitely commit himself: his words as to 'certain ancient writers' may be taken as referring merely to the exact site of the grave in the cemetery. But we have seen that in the last days of the abbey the monks expressed doubt on the matter. We have also referred to the royal writ which granted permission for a search in 1345. The writ is printed from the Patent Roll in Rymer's *Foedera* (v. 458). It is sufficiently curious to be quoted here.

The King to all to whom these presents shall come, greeting.
John Blome of London has petitioned us that since (as he asserts) a divine injunction has been laid on him as concerning

the venerable body of the noble decurion Joseph of Arimathea, which rests in Christ buried within the bounds of the monastery of Glastonbury, and is to be revealed in these days to the honour [of God?] and the edification of many; to wit, that he should seek it diligently until he find it; because it is said to be contained in certain ancient writings that his body was there buried: We therefore (if so it be) desiring to pay devout honour to his sepulchre and to the relics of him who performed such offices of religion and humanity to our Redeemer in His death, taking down His body from the cross and laying it in his own new sepulchre; and hoping for ourselves and all our realm a wealth of grace from the revelation aforesaid; Have conceded and licence given, so far as rests with us, to the said John that he should have power to dig within the precinct of the said monastery and seek for those precious relics according to the injunction and the revelation made to him in the places where he shall see it to be most suitable: Provided however that this can be done without hurt to our beloved in Christ the abbot and convent of the said monastery and without destruction of their church and houses there; and that for this purpose he have the licence and assent of the abbot and convent themselves.

In testimony whereof, &c. Witness the King at Westminster, on the tenth day of June. By the King himself.

Whether the licence of the abbot and convent was obtained, whether the search was made and proved fruitless, we do not know. We have indeed the statement of an anonymous East Anglian chronicler, who has the brief entry under the year 1367, 'The bodies of Joseph of Arimathea and his companions were found at Glastonbury.' The chronicle was printed by Sparke (*Scriptores*, 1, 137), who assigned this part of it to one John of Boston. Liebermann however investigated it in detail in the *Neues Archiv* for 1892 (XVIII, 235–245), and decided that it was all one work, of the latter part of the fourteenth century, anonymous, but showing connexion with both Peterborough and Spalding.

A notice such as this from so great a distance is of no value against the silence of Glastonbury itself. It may be

PLATE VII

AT SHARPHAM MANOR

a belated rumour based on the royal writ of twenty years before. It is just possible that search was again being made by the monks themselves, and that tidings of this leaked out. If the search had been successful, we should not have been left in doubt regarding it.

V

The Two Cruets of St Joseph of Arimathea

1. The heraldic shield bearing a cross between two cruets was much employed, if not first introduced, by Richard Bere, the last abbot but one (1494–1524). Warner (*Glastonbury*, p. 268) speaks of 'an escutcheon charged with R. Bere's fanciful arms—a cross between two beer-flagons'!

It is to be seen in sixteenth-century glass, as we have said (p. 49), in the south window of the chancel of St John's Church. In stone it occurs frequently, as, for example:

(1) On the battlement of the north aisle of the church of St Benignus, built by this abbot, immediately above the north porch: here are also the initials 'R. B.'

(2) On the outside of the east wall of the chapel of Abbot Bere's almshouses.

(3) At the back of the manor house built by this abbot at Sharpham Park, near Glastonbury.

(4) According to Collinson (II, 262) a house in Glastonbury built in 1714 was adorned with various arms taken from the abbey ruins, among others being 'a cross between two cups.'

2. In the east window of Langport Church there is a figure, with the name of St Joseph of Arimathea beneath it, in the lowest panel on the south side. This beautiful glass has been skilfully brought together from various parts of the church, and may be dated fifteenth or sixteenth century. St Joseph carries the two cruets on a white cloth in his right hand.

On the chancel screen of the church of Plymtree, near Cullompton, Devon, is a similar representation of the saint with his two cruets.

VI

William Good's Narrative

The original Latin of this interesting passage, with the exception of the last paragraph, was printed by Archbishop Ussher in his *Antiquitates* (p. 16 of ed. 1687). The reference there given for it is 'Edvard. Maihew Congregat. Anglican. ordinis Benedict. Tabula. 2. pag. 1118, 1119.' By a strange coincidence the copies of this work in the British Museum, in the Bodleian Library, and in the Library of Trinity College, Dublin, are all imperfect and do not contain this particular passage. There is however a complete copy in Archbishop Marsh's Library in Dublin.

Maihew's *Trophaea* is divided into three *Tabulae*; but the numbering of the pages is continuous throughout, so that the second *Tabula* contains pp. 883–1888. Dr White, the Librarian of Archbishop Marsh's Library, writes: 'Our copy must have come from Stillingfleet's collection, which Marsh purchased about 1704.' I owe to his courtesy and that of his son, Mr N. B. White, a transcript of the passage, from which some portions not given by Ussher may be quoted here, beginning with the account of William Good.

Hic enim in eodem Monasterio cum adhuc in florente statu consisteret, puer ut missae sacrificio inserviret enutritus, illo subverso regnante Catholica Regina Maria, Sacerdos; Catholicos autem persequente Regina Elizabetha, Societatis Jesu religiosus est factus. Cumque Romae collegii Anglicani Ecclesia imaginibus ornaretur, ipse imprimis praecipuorum Angliae Sanctorum Catalogum collegit, authorque fuit, ut ipsorum imagines resque gestae ibidem coloribus iuxta histor-iarum veritatem exprimerentur. De Glasconiensi autem coenobio Sanctoque Josepho ab Arimathaea quae sequuntur propria manu scripta proprioque nomine subsignata ibidem reliquit. 'Glasconiae exstabant (inquit)...[so on as in *Ussher* to]...sepultus esse. Fuit ibidem sacellum subterraneum longum quo fiebat famosissima peregrinatio ad imaginem saxeam hujus Sancti, & multa miracula, etiam me puero, qui ibi natus sum, & servivi sacello puer octennis, & vidi destrui ab impio viro Gulielmo Goals sub Henrico octavo.' *Hactenus sunt ipsius verba*; quibus propria manu nomen suum ut diximus subscripsit: haecque ego ex ipsomet authographo cum Romae eiusdem collegii Anglicani alumnus agerem, exscripsi mecumque per mare, per terras, inter saevissimas haereticorum persequutiones semper salva tutatus sum. Quod autem ad montem illum Hamdenhil nuncupatum, in quo aliqui S. Josephum ab Arimathaea sepultum perhibent, spectat, habebatur sane olim sacellum in illo monte constructum inter sacra & veneranda Angliae loca. Memini vero cum aliquando per illum montem ipse transirem, me a fide dignis accepisse, senem quemdam qui non longe ab eo loco habitabat, saepius, regnante Elizabetha haeretica, illum locum visitare, ibique certo in loco flexis genibus orare solitum.

VII

On the Names of some Glastonbury Monks

An interesting document has recently been published by the *Somerset Record Society* (vol. xxxix, 'Collectanea,' p. 210), entitled 'Visitation of Religious Houses and Hospitals 1526.' The date is two years after Richard Whiting's accession. The names of the abbot and fifty monks are given. A study of the list offers a new illustration of the vogue of the Arthurian legend in Abbot Bere's day.

The elder monks nearly all take their surnames after the usual fashion from the places of their birth or residence. Thomas Dunston, twelfth on the list, is an exception. But after four more names derived from places, a new type of nomenclature prevails. The name of a saint or local hero is used as the surname in nearly thirty instances. Among these the following are of special interest:

> Robertus Armathie and Johannes Limathie (?)[1]
> Johannes Arthure
> Robertus Ider
> Willelmus Yosephe.

Other names which have come before us in our discussion are represented by

Robertus Gylde	Martinus Indracte
Johannes Patricius	Johannes Fagan.

There is a similar change from place-names to saints' names among the younger monks at Athelney; and the two juniors at Muchelney shew that the habit was spreading in the neighbourhood. But this particular group of names is, as we might expect, peculiar to Glastonbury.

---

[1] This appears to correspond with the *Abaramathia* of the signatures to the acknowledgment of the royal supremacy; see the 7th Report of the Deputy Keeper of Public Records, p. 287. The list there given shews also a 'Johannes Derynyian'—evidently for 'Deruvian.'

Printed in the United States
By Bookmasters